THE GREAT PHYSICIAN'S

R^x *for*

HIGH CHOLESTEROL

JORDAN RUBIN

with Joseph Brasco, M.D.

THOMAS NELSON
Since 1798

NASHVILLE   DALLAS   MEXICO CITY   RIO DE JANEIRO   BEIJING

Every effort has been made to make this book as accurate as possible. The purpose of this book is to educate. It is a review of scientific evidence that is presented for information purposes. No individual should use the information in this book for self-diagnosis, treatment, or justification in accepting or declining any medical therapy for any health problems or diseases. No individual is discouraged from seeking professional medical advice and treatment, and this book is not supplying medical advice.

Any application of the information herein is at the reader's own discretion and risk. Therefore, any individual with a specific health problem or who is taking medications must first seek advice from his personal physician or health-care provider before starting a health and wellness program. The author and Thomas Nelson Publishers, Inc., shall have neither liability nor responsibility to any person or entity with respect to loss, damage, or injury caused or alleged to be caused directly or indirectly by the information contained in this book. We assume no responsibility for errors, inaccuracies, omissions, or any inconsistency herein.

In view of the complex, individual nature of health problems, this book, and the ideas, programs, procedures, and suggestions herein are not intended to replace the advice of trained medical professionals. All matters regarding one's health require medical supervision. A physician should be consulted prior to adopting any program or programs described in this book. The author and publisher disclaim any liability arising directly or indirectly from the use of this book.

Published in Nashville, Tennessee. Thomas Nelson is a trademark of Thomas Nelson, Inc.

Thomas Nelson Inc. titles may be purchased in bulk for educational, business, fundraising, or sales promotional use. For information, please e-mail SpecialMarkets@ThomasNelson.com.

Scripture quotations are taken from THE NEW KING JAMES VERSION. Copyright © 1982 by Thomas Nelson, Inc. Used by permission. All rights reserved.

Library of Congress Cataloging-in-Publication Data

Rubin, Jordan.
    The Great Physician's Rx for high cholesterol / by Jordan Rubin with Joseph Brasco.
      p. cm.
    Includes bibliographical references.
    ISBN-10: 0-7852-1948-X (hardcover)
    ISBN-13: 978-0-7852-1948-X (hardcover)
    1. Heartburn and Acid Reflux—Popular works. 2. Heartburn and Acid Reflux—Religious aspects—Christianity. 3. Heartburn and Acid Reflux—Rehabilitation—Popular works.
I. Brasco, Joseph. II. Title.
RC660.4.R84 2006
616.4'6206—dc22
                                           2005036830

Printed in the United States of America

07 08 09 10 QW 6 5 4 3 2 1

CONTENTS

iii

INTRODUCTION

Down for the Count

Carol Wootten grew up in the Central California community of Watsonville, an agricultural settlement whose civic fathers christened the "Strawberry Capitol of the World." Every August, Watsonville plays host to the Monterey Bay Strawberry Festival, which attracts tens of thousands annually to sample an array of strawberry-flavored treats (including strawberry tamales!), participate in strawberry pie–eating contests, and enjoy the Miss Monterey Bay Strawberry Queen Pageant.

Carol's father, Ken Miller, didn't want to work in the strawberry fields forever (sorry, bad pun), so he performed a variety of odd jobs: police officer, ambulance driver, and shift worker at Martinelli's apple juice and cider plant in Watsonville. The Miller refrigerator was always filled with dark green bottles of the sparkling cider. "I drank a lot of Martinelli's growing up," Carol said.

Sipping sugary apple cider wasn't the main reason why Carol gained weight as she progressed into high school. She was just a larger-than-average girl. "I weighed around two hundred pounds, and that bothered me, but something my doctor said really helped. He told me, 'God made each one of us individuals, so don't worry too much about what you weigh. As long as you're healthy—and you are—then you're okay.'" After that, Carol was comfortable in her own skin, although she still wanted to lose some weight for appearance's sake. She ate Weight Watchers meals to reduce caloric intake, but she could never make any weight loss stick.

When Carol turned twenty-one in 1978, she married Edward Wootten and moved to Charleston, South Carolina, where Ed was stationed in the US Navy. Their only child, Jeremy, arrived three years later, and after that event, she didn't care any more what she put into her body. She would grab crackers, chips, or a half gallon of ice cream whenever the desire hit.

She took her first cholesterol test during her pregnancy. Her LDL cholesterol level—the low-density lipoprotein or "bad" cholesterol that doctors watch closely because it can build up inside arterial walls—was in the low hundreds, which was optimal. But when she submitted to her next cholesterol test eight or nine years later, her LDL levels had shot up to 180, which put her squarely in the "High" category, according to tables from the National Heart, Lung, and Blood Institute.

"You need to start watching what you eat," her doctor counseled her. "Especially the red meat."

Carol wasn't happy to hear that advice. She *loved* hamburgers. Whenever she sat down in a restaurant or passed through a fast-food joint, she always ordered a juicy burger and fries. Pepperoni pizza was another favorite, but after learning that she had high cholesterol, Carol ate more chicken and fish, although "there were not a lot of fish that I liked," she said.

A subsequent cholesterol test put her LDL levels at 185, and that number remained high as her health deteriorated in her late forties. Meanwhile, her weight ballooned past three hundred pounds. Since diet and lifestyle weren't turning her cholesterol numbers in a positive direction, her doctor recommended that she start taking a cholesterol-reducing drug called Niaspan.

Niaspan is an extended-release form of niacin that has been found to reduce blood cholesterol levels and combat clogged arteries. Its literature states, however, that this prescription drug "is not for everyone" because of side effects that range from liver damage to dizziness to "flushing," which is a feeling of warmth on the neck, ears, and face.

"I didn't like the way Niaspan made me feel because of the flushing," Carol said. "I felt like my whole body was on fire for around twenty minutes. The warmth and redness on my skin felt like a bad sunburn." Niaspan did push her LDL cholesterol levels down to 154, however.

And that's where her cholesterol level stayed for several months until a staph infection in her left knee robbed her of her ability to walk or move around. After being hospitalized, her condition became so serious that she nearly died when her vital signs bottomed out. Fortunately for Carol, she experienced a miracle and was given a new lease on life. (I'll share more about this part of Carol's story in "Key #7: Live a Life of Prayer and Purpose.")

A few months after Carol was released from the hospital, I was invited to share the message of the Great Physician's prescription at Calvary Temple Worship Center in Modesto, California, not far from where Carol and her husband now reside. The pastoral team and congregation responded so well to the message that Calvary Temple hosted a "7 Weeks of Wellness" challenge to take the health of their church to the next level. More than 360 men and women participated, including Carol Wootten. Each week, men and women listened as Kelli Williams, the health ministries pastor and a registered nurse, facilitated the program utilizing our 7 Weeks of Wellness church curriculum.

"When I heard you speak at Calvary Temple, it was like a light went off," Carol said. "I was forty-eight years old, and I figured if I didn't do something real quick, I wasn't going to make it to age fifty. I didn't feel well, had no energy, and felt like a lump. That's probably because I ate what I wanted to eat when I wanted to eat."

Carol listened to my advice to eat foods that God created instead of man-made foods that make up the bulk of the standard American diet (SAD). She changed her diet and began consuming fresh, healthy foods at set, regular mealtimes. Snacking on junk food was out. "My whole family switched over," she said. "Nothing came into our house that wasn't good for us."

After two months of following the Great Physician's prescription, Carol's LDL cholesterol count dropped from 154 to 91! After two more months, she had lost thirty-four pounds! But more important, Carol requested and received permission from her doctor to cut her Niaspan prescription way back. Instead of taking the drug daily, she ingests the drug only twice a week.

"I hope to be completely off Niaspan soon, but I think following the Great Physician's prescription for eating did a lot more to lower my cholesterol levels than taking a prescription drug," Carol said. "I can say this because I immediately noticed a dramatic change in the way I felt and in my cholesterol levels after I started eating the right foods and living a healthy lifestyle."

COUNTING UP CHOLESTEROL

A story like Carol Wootten's warms my heart and shows that the Great Physician's prescription can help assure healthy cholesterol levels in the body. Cholesterol, like controversial NFL wide receiver Terrell Owens, carries a bad boy reputation in our culture. Since the phrases "high cholesterol" and "heart disease" are linked so closely in the public's mind, people tend to view cholesterol in negative terms—like a killer of the masses. Because of the bad press, few are aware that every single cell in your body *needs* cholesterol.

The plain truth is that our bodies wouldn't survive very long without this soft, waxlike substance produced by the liver and found in the bloodstream and all of the body's cells. Cholesterol is the source material for various hormones such as estrogen and testosterone, is necessary for cell membranes, and is needed for proper brain and nerve function. Most of the cholesterol in your body does *not* come from the foods you eat: most people receive 200 to 500 milligrams of cholesterol from foods such as meats, poultry, fish, eggs, butter, cheese, and whole milk. Meanwhile, the liver produces around 1,000 milligrams of cholesterol daily.

Cholesterol is transported in the bloodstream by lipoproteins—actually, a pair of different ones. A high-density lipoprotein (HDL) is known as the "good" cholesterol because it collects unused cholesterol and transports it back to the liver, where it is destroyed or sent back out to the body as needed. A low-density lipoprotein (LDL) is known as Public Enemy No. 1, however, because this bad cholesterol builds up and clings to the inside of the arteries. Medical researchers have learned that large numbers of LDL particles are strongly associated with coronary heart disease, but elevated cholesterol may actually be a sign of antioxidant deficiency in the body because the liver makes cholesterol to help seal the cracks in arteries caused by oxidation.

The issue at hand—and the reason I'm writing this book—is that too many Americans have too much cholesterol swirling in their bloodstreams. Approximately 37 million adults in this country have high blood cholesterol counts, and 105 million—*half* the US adult population—have cholesterol levels that are higher than desirable, according to the Mayo Clinic.[1] Looked at another way, since there were 105 million households in the last U.S. Census in 2000, this effectively means that every household in the country could conceivably have one person living under its roof with a cholesterol level that's unacceptably high.

In medical terms, the genesis of high cholesterol begins when the levels of cholesterol and triglycerides, a blood fat, become too high in your bloodstream. This causes the development of cholesterol-containing fatty deposits—known as plaque—to form and begin traveling through your blood vessels. Over time, plaque can clog your arteries and veins like sludge in a drainpipe.

What Do the Trends Show?

Cholesterol levels are going down for middle-aged to older adults, but not for their adult children, according to Minnesota researchers who undertook a twenty-year survey of the incidence of high cholesterol. The Minnesota Heart Study, released in 2005, found that men forty-five years and older had the highest cholesterol levels back in the early 1980s.

In the most recent survey taken from 2000 to 2002, however, men ages thirty-five to forty-four had the highest cholesterol levels, and younger men and women ages twenty-five to thirty-four showed larger percentage increases in cholesterol levels. The lead author of the study, Donna K. Arnett, Ph.D., at the University of Alabama at Birmingham, said older people's cholesterol levels have decreased because of their increased use of cholesterol-reducing medications like Lipitor, while young adults aren't paying close attention to their diets and lifestyle.[2]

When arteries traveling to the heart become partially blocked, this creates a condition known as atherosclerosis. For healthy individuals, blood rushes through their arteries like traffic on an empty turnpike, but when plaque deposits build up and stick to the artery wall lining, that's the equivalent of merging three lanes down to a single lane. Blood flow to the heart is greatly reduced, which prevents the body's cardiovascular system from getting as much oxygen-rich blood as it needs. When blood flow is reduced even by a small amount, you feel chest pain, also known as angina. When a blood clot suddenly cuts off all or nearly all of the blood supply, the heart muscle is starved for oxygen. Within a short time, the death of heart muscle cells occurs—the official start of a myocardial infarction, or heart attack.

Death by heart attacks or lingering cardiovascular diseases (CVD) is this country's number one killer, claiming more lives than all other leading causes of death, according to the American Heart Association's latest compilation of *Heart Disease and Stroke Statistics*. A total of 927,448 Americans died from various cardiovascular diseases in 2002, the most recent year that data are available.[3] Cardiovascular diseases include high blood pressure, coronary heart disease (heart attacks and angina), congestive heart failure, strokes, and congenital heart defects.

Modern medicine often points to high cholesterol, along with high blood pressure, as the major cause of cardiovascular disease. For example, the Mayo Clinic reported that half of all heart disease deaths each year can be attributed to high cholesterol, but I feel that blaming high cholesterol for producing arterial damage is like blaming the fireman for the fire. Renowned heart surgeon Dr. Michael DeBakey, who directed the Cardiovascular Research and Training Center in Houston, said that thirty years of observing more than fifteen thousand patients had led him to conclude that cholesterol was not the central cause of atherosclerosis, the artery-clogging condition that kills hundreds of thousands of Americans each year.[4]

Dr. DeBakey put the number of coronary artery disease victims with high blood cholesterol at 30 to 40 percent. "If you say cholesterol is the cause, how do you explain the other 60 percent

to 70 percent with heart disease who don't have high cholesterol?"
he wondered.[5]

Good question—no, make that a *great* question.

CONVENTIONAL MEDICINE

Most people don't know they have high cholesterol—which
doesn't manifest itself through any noticeable symptoms—
until they submit themselves to a routine blood test given during an annual checkup or life insurance examination. Within
a day or two, the results come back from the lab with cholesterol levels measured in milligrams (mg) of cholesterol per
deciliter (dl) of blood. According to the National Heart, Lung,
and Blood Institute, these are the numbers you want to see:

TOTAL SERUM CHOLESTEROL
(INCLUDING LDL AND HDL NUMBERS)

- below 200 mg/dl: desirable
- 200–239 mg/dl: borderline high
- 240 mg/dl and above: high

HDL CHOLESTEROL LEVELS ("GOOD" CHOLESTEROL)

- below 40 mg/dl: bad
- 40–59 mg/dl: better
- 60 mg/dl and above: best

LDL Cholesterol Levels ("Bad" Cholesterol)

- below 100 mg/dl: optimal
- 100–129 mg/dl: near optimal
- 130–159 mg/dl: borderline high
- 160–189 mg/dl: high
- 190 mg/dl and above: very high

During a routine life insurance exam recently, my total cholesterol level was 160—well beneath 200, which is considered borderline high. I attribute that good number to following the advice I put forth in the Great Physician's prescription as well as my youth, since I'm currently thirty-one years old.

Family physicians understand that the most likely candidates for high cholesterol are overweight men and women over the age of fifty complaining of general health malaise. Sometimes a notation in a chart can trip a doctor's suspicion: a family history of heart disease before the age of fifty-five; someone who smokes or lives with family members who light up; or a patient who looks out of shape or recently experienced major weight gain.

The results of cholesterol testing speak for themselves since the numbers are fairly cut and dried. Doctors don't like to see an HDL measurement of 40 mg/dl or lower or a number higher than 160 mg/dl for LDL cholesterol. When those numbers present themselves, physicians are thinking, *This person is a ticking time bomb.* They are aware that conventional wisdom states that if their patient can drop the LDL level by 1 percent, there will be a corresponding 2 percent drop in the risk of heart attack. By the same token, for every 1 percent increase in HDL levels, the risk of heart attack drops by 3 to 4 percent.[6]

Most doctors suggest making lifestyle changes since they believe that a poor cholesterol test result reflects the level of risk for developing coronary heart disease. They will direct you to change your diet and begin exercising to bring your cholesterol levels—and weight—down to a more manageable number. You may be told that the National Cholesterol Education guidelines suggest at least a six-month program of eating less saturated fats before resorting to drug therapy. You may be given a list of some of your favorite foods to avoid: hamburgers and hot dogs, eggs, butter, ice cream, pie, white bread, fried foods, and coffee. The thought of watching everyone else enjoy a Fourth of July cookout while you're eating a salad doesn't sound like fun, nor does forgoing your favorite latte on your way to work. (I'll have more to say about this dietary advice in the next chapter, "Key #1: Eat to Live.")

More often than not, I'm afraid, even patients who've been "good" return for a six-month checkup with nearly the same cholesterol numbers. When that happens, physicians routinely reach for their prescription pads and prescribe a cholesterol-lowering drug known as a statin. In 2005, doctors nearly got writer's cramp from filling out 150 million prescriptions for statin drugs.[7]

Statin drugs interrupt the formation of cholesterol inside the body by prompting the liver to block a substance the body needs to produce cholesterol while helping the body reabsorb cholesterol that has accumulated in plaques clinging to your arterial walls. Commonly prescribed statins include:

- Lipitor (atorvastatin)
- Pravachol (pravastatin)
- Lescol (fluvastatin)
- Mevacor (lovastatin)
- Crestor (rosuvastatin calcium)
- Zocor (simvastatin)

I would imagine that you recognize the first statin drug on this list: Lipitor. Racking up $13 billion in sales in 2006, Lipitor is the best-selling drug in the world and a cash cow for Pfizer, the maker of Viagra. If you happen to be forty years old or older (and especially a male), submit to an annual physical, have blood drawn, and learn that you have a total cholesterol level higher than 200, your family physician will probably write you a prescription for Lipitor. It's practically automatic these days and one reason why twelve million Americans, or 4 percent of the US population, are swallowing this cholesterol-lowering drug with their morning OJ. Lipitor is not cheap: most pay around seven hundred to eight hundred dollars a year for their meds.

It's difficult to tell how many Americans consume cholesterol-reducing drugs on a daily basis, but some in the medical establishment think that market is underserved. Benjamin M. Scirica, M.D., and Christopher P. Cannon, M.D., writing in *Circulation* (the journal of the American Heart Association) on behalf of their cardiovascular research work at Brigham and Women's Hospital in Boston, had this to say:

As we age, cholesterol builds up in the arteries of the heart and neck, placing us at risk for heart attacks, strokes, and premature death. Treatment that lowers cholesterol in the blood has therefore become the cornerstone of prevention of future heart attack, stroke, and death, both in persons who definitely have heart disease and in those who are at risk of developing it in the future.

Evidence suggests that millions of people who could benefit from cholesterol-lowering medicines are currently untreated. According to the American Heart Association, nearly thirty-eight million patients in the United States would benefit from the combination of diet and drug therapy, and an additional thirty million should follow diet and exercise programs to reduce cholesterol levels. Unfortunately, cholesterol-lowering treatment is widely underutilized because of the lack of awareness, fear of side effects, reluctance of otherwise healthy people to take medication, and cost.[8]

No one doubts that Lipitor and its statin cousins are potent medicines that usually reduce cholesterol levels, but at what financial and health costs? Regarding the latter, the so-called minor side effects are nausea, diarrhea, constipation, and muscle aches. Two potentially serious side effects are elevated liver enzymes (medicalese for liver damage) and statin myopathy (medicalese for kidney failure).

Another bad side effect is death. A statin called Baycol, introduced by the German pharmaceutical firm Bayer in 1998, was pulled from the market by the Food and Drug Administration in 2001 after the drug was allegedly linked to the deaths of thirty-one patients who developed a disorder called rhabdomyolysis, in which muscle cells break down and flood the kidneys with cellular waste. The problems with Baycol caught many by surprise. Charlotte Collins of Havelock, North Carolina, told the *New York Times*, "I was standing up and just raising my foot to put on my pants, and my back gave out on me. The muscles stopped working."[9] Those who perished died when their kidneys were overwhelmed and shut down.

Despite the possibility—no matter how remote—that someone could die from taking a medication, I understand why physicians write so many prescriptions for statin drugs: it's easier to hand over a prescription than to teach the patient how to live a healthy lifestyle. If you are on statin drugs (or have taken them in the past), it's not my place to advise you on whether you should continue taking these medications in the future. I am confident, though, that following the Great Physician's prescription for high cholesterol will give you an opportunity to live a longer, healthier life, and I believe following this program may give you an opportunity to flush those cholesterol-reducing drugs down the toilet—under a doctor's supervision, of course.

ALTERNATIVE TREATMENTS

The alternative medical approach to treating high cholesterol revolves around the use of vitamins, minerals, amino acids, herbs, and other biological compounds as natural substitutes to prescription drugs like Lipitor. Gugulipid is extracted from the mukul myrrh tree, native to India. *The Encyclopedia of Natural*

Medicine reports that several studies have confirmed gugulipid has an ability to lower both cholesterol and triglyceride levels at rates comparable to cholesterol-reducing drugs—but without the attendant side effects.[10]

Some favor red rice yeast, which is reputed to lower cholesterol levels because it contains naturally occurring lovastatin, a similar compound to the most popular statin drugs on the market today. Plant sterols and stanols, which are substances that are naturally found in many grains, vegetables, fruits, legumes, nuts, and seeds, have powerful cholesterol-lowering properties. The sterols and stanols prevent cholesterol from foods being absorbed in your bloodstream.

Acupressure, a traditional Chinese medicine technique, involves placing physical pressure by hand or elbow on different pressure points on the surface of the body to bring about relief through greater balance and circulation of fluids. Proponents believe that acupressure can be helpful in keeping blood flowing to the heart and chest.

In researching this book, I found it interesting how few alternative treatments there were for high cholesterol. I think that's because the traditional medical community and alternative medical practitioners agree that lifestyle changes in diet and exercise go a long way toward pushing those HDL and LDL numbers in the right direction.

A ROAD MAP FROM HERE

If your doctor has informed you that your cholesterol test came back with results that put you in the unacceptably high category, you should regard that information as you view a red "engine warning" light on the dashboard of your car. Sure, you can keep the car running a while longer, and you may not even notice a reduction in performance. But signs of high cholesterol are a warning light for serious potential future health problems: gallstones, high blood pressure, impotence, heart disease, and stroke.

What are you going to do about the red warning light in your peripheral vision?

Reading *The Great Physician's Rx for High Cholesterol* is a good place to start. I believe high cholesterol is highly preventable and even reversible if you take hold of the seven keys presented in this book. Yes, following these seven keys involves lifestyle changes, but if you're eating like a pig, drinking like a fish, and smoking like a chimney, then you're just as much a walking time bomb as Carol Wootten ever was. If your idea of exercise is walking into a McDonald's instead of using the drive-through window, then I would make sure your life insurance is paid up because each year, each month, and each morning is a roll of the dice.

The seven keys to unlock the body's healthy potential, established in my foundational book, *The Great Physician's Rx for Health and Wellness* are:

- Key #1: Eat to Live

- Key #2: Supplement Your Diet with Whole Food Nutritionals, Living Nutrients, and Superfoods

- Key #3: Practice Advanced Hygiene

- Key #4: Condition Your Body with Exercise and Body Therapies
- Key #5: Reduce Toxins in Your Environment
- Key #6: Avoid Deadly Emotions
- Key #7: Live a Life of Prayer and Purpose

Each of these keys should directly support your goal to minimize the effects of high cholesterol in your life. My main goal for writing *The Great Physician's Rx for High Cholesterol* is to give you a "prevent defense," to use a football term. Incorporating these timeless principles will allow the living God to transform your health as you honor Him physically, mentally, emotionally, and spiritually.

Since you're reading this book, I figure that you've noticed that red warning light and you're motivated to do something about it. If so, please know that I've written *The Great Physician's Rx for High Cholesterol* for you. Following the seven keys will supply you with the energy you need to attack the day, be there for your kids, and fulfill God's purpose for your life.

Please understand that the Great Physician's Rx for high cholesterol is not guaranteed to lower your cholesterol levels, and I would never want anyone to represent this book as promising a "cure" to this potentially life-threatening condition. My great hope is that the seven keys will do one of two things for you:

1. Give you the best possible chance to get control of the amount of cholesterol in your bloodstream, increase antioxidant levels, and live a long, healthy life.

2. Give you the chance to get off cholesterol-reducing mediations like Lipitor and Zocor.

Sound like a plan? If so, let's get started.

KEY #1

Eat to Live

Growing up in cosmopolitan Copenhagen in the aftermath of World War II, Uffe Ravnskov set out to become a doctor. His dream was realized at the University of Copenhagen in 1961, when he received his M.D. and began his clinical education in various hospitals in Denmark and Sweden. Dr. Ravnskov was an inquisitive sort who devoted years of research to heart aneurysms, heart attacks, and urinary tract infections. He gathered a reputation as a contrarian who didn't automatically accept the prevailing conventional wisdom: for instance, when his research into the major cause of urinary tract infections in women turned out to be soap, not bacteria, he wasn't afraid to publish a paper in the medical journal saying so.

In the late 1980s, the Swedish equivalent of the American Medical Association began beating the cholesterol drum to warn everyone from Stockholm to Stocksätter about the dangers of eating foods high in dietary fat because of its association with the development of high cholesterol and cardiovascular diseases. By golly, the Swedes were going to do something about the rising number of heart attacks in their country, even if that meant changing the Swedish attitude about eating a Danish in the morning.

At this time, Dr. Ravnskov oversaw a busy practice in southern Sweden. One of his patients was Karen, a cheerful and optimistic sixty-two-year-old woman who cleaned offices in a nearby factory. When Karen made an appointment to see Dr. Ravnskov, he noticed that his formerly chipper patient was tired and depressed, not at all her old self.

Dr. Ravnskov gently inquired why she wasn't feeling well. She replied that two years earlier her company had asked all the employees to participate in a series of health exams, including blood tests. Her cholesterol count came back too high, Karen said. The company doctor informed her that she was a likely candidate to have a heart attack within five years if she didn't change her diet.

Only five years to live! The news shook Karen because she felt fit as a fiddle and was looking forward to an energetic retirement. When she asked what she could do to extend her life, the company doctor directed her to stop eating high-fat foods and turn to a low-fat, high-fiber diet of fruits and vegetables. This advice distressed Karen, who loved to cook and was known in her village as the maker of the best cheesecake north of Amsterdam.

Karen accepted the company doctor's advice, though lifelong habits were hard to break. If she and her husband celebrated a special occasion with a steak, she trimmed off all the fat, even though it was the "tasty and best part," she said. Despite drastically modifying her diet, however, her high cholesterol levels did not budge. After reviewing her chart, the company doctor informed her that she wasn't doing enough. "You need pills," he declared, so he wrote Karen a prescription for cholesterol-reducing drugs.

The medications made her feel even *worse*. Nausea and physical discomfort would strike within an hour of gulping down the pills. Her appetite disappeared, and she didn't want to eat anything at all. Karen lost weight, but more distressing, she lost her stamina and zest for life.

The combination of diet and drugs did lower her cholesterol some but not enough to satisfy the company dietician, who regarded Karen with great skepticism when she promised that she had been eating right. "That's impossible," the dietician scolded. "You must have eaten more fat than that."

Karen felt terribly guilty because she had enjoyed a piece of her favorite dessert—cheesecake—the night before.[1]

Chances are that if you're dealing with high cholesterol, you feel guilty when you dig into some of your favorite comfort foods. If so, you're not alone. In his book, *The Cholesterol Myths,* Dr. Ravnskov described the results of a Gallup Poll taken in this country showing that 56 percent of all Americans worry about fat and cholesterol, 45 percent think that the food they like is not good for them, and 36 percent have guilt feelings when they eat the foods they like.[2]

The reason we feel this way is that physicians have a way of putting the fear of God into their patients when it comes to diet, as Karen and Carol Wootten can attest. Doctors will bluntly tell you to lay off barbecued steak, stop eating hamburgers, stay away from deep-dish pizza, shake your salt habit, substitute a margarine spread for butter, and say no to nuts. They will outline a strict diet that puts many of your favorite foods off-limits—no cheese, butter, or other full-fat dairy products—with orders to eat lots of fish, small amounts of lean meat, and plenty of high-fiber fruits and vegetables.

The reason physicians impart this dietary advice stems from

an entrenched, widely held belief that has been part of modern medicine for decades: a high-cholesterol diet promotes coronary heart disease, and the best way to *prevent* heart disease is for patients to restrict their diet to low-fat, high-fiber foods.

The diet-heart connection, as it's known in the hallways of our nation's medical schools, has become one of the most deeply ingrained beliefs in modern medicine. The scientific link between high cholesterol levels and cardiovascular disease dates back to a landmark research project called the Framingham Heart Study, which began in 1948 when researchers recruited 5,209 men and women between the ages of thirty and sixty-two from the town of Framingham, Massachusetts.

The objective of the Framingham Heart Study—it's still going strong after nearly sixty years—is to identify the common factors or characteristics that contribute to cardiovascular disease by following its development over a long period of time in a large group of participants who had not yet developed overt symptoms of CVD or suffered a heart attack or stroke. A project of the National Heart, Lung, and Blood Institute, the Framingham Heart Study is on its third generational cohort of participants.

The thousands of Framingham residents who have participated in the study have submitted to extensive physical examinations and lifestyle interviews, which have been analyzed for common patterns related to cardiovascular disease development. In 1961, the Framingham Heart Study announced one of its first major discoveries: cholesterol level abnormalities were found to increase the risk of heart disease. Other research milestones followed: in 1987, high blood cholesterol levels were found to correlate directly with the risk of death in young men; and in 1988, high levels of good HDL cholesterol were found to reduce the risk of death.

One doctor closely following the scientific literature about the latest research coming from the Framingham Heart Study was Dr. Ravnskov, who earned a Ph.D. for his scientific studies at the Departments of Nephrology and Clinical Chemistry at the University Hospital in Lund, Sweden, during the 1970s before starting his private practice.

Remember, Dr. Ravnskov likes to think outside the medical box, and he wasn't convinced that cholesterol hardens arteries while carrying vital oxygen and nutrients to and from the heart. The more Dr. Ravnskov evaluated the Framingham Heart Study and other peer-review studies in top American medical journals, the more he believed that the case against cholesterol was built on circumstantial evidence. From Dr. Ravnskov's viewpoint, the emperor—King Cholesterol—wore no clothes because as best as he could determine, he couldn't find conclusive proof regarding the connection between high cholesterol levels and cardiovascular disease. The Swedish doctor wrote nearly forty medical papers critical of the alleged association between cholesterol and cardiovascular disease.

For instance, he pointed out that in a thirty-year follow-up of the Framingham population, high cholesterol wasn't predictive for a heart attack after the age of forty-seven, and those whose cholesterol went down actually had the biggest risk of having a heart attack! His citation came straight from the Framingham study: "For each 1 mg/dl drop of cholesterol, there was an 11 percent *increase* [italics added for emphasis] in coronary and total mortality."

The World of Cholesterol According to Dr. Ravnskov

Dr. Uffe Ravnskov makes a lot of sense to me. Here are seven key points that outline his views on cholesterol:

1. Cholesterol is not a deadly poison but a vital substance found in every cell membrane. There is no such thing as "good" or "bad" cholesterol; mental stress, physical activity, and change of body weight may influence the level of blood cholesterol. High cholesterol is not dangerous by itself, but it may reflect an unhealthy condition.

2. High blood cholesterol is said to promote coronary heart disease, but many studies have shown that people whose blood cholesterol is low become just as prone to coronary heart disease as people whose cholesterol is high.

3. Your body produces three to four times *more* cholesterol than you eat. The production of cholesterol can increase when you eat little cholesterol and can decrease when you eat much. Even the best low-cholesterol diets cannot be counted on to lower cholesterol levels by more than a few percentage points.

4. There is no evidence that too much animal fat and cholesterol in the diet promote atherosclerosis or heart attacks. For instance, more than twenty studies have shown that people who have had heart attacks haven't eaten more fat than other people, and the degree of atherosclerosis discovered at their autopsies was unrelated to their diets.

5. Many researchers and doctors claim that the only effective way to lower cholesterol is with drugs, but statin drugs like Lipitor are dangerous to your health and may shorten your life.

6. Many of the facts in this list have been presented in scientific journals and books for decades, but the proponents of the diet-heart theory rarely convey these facts to the public.

7. The reason why medical doctors and researchers, as well as laymen, have been misled is that opposing and disagreeing results are systematically ignored or misquoted in the scientific press.[3]

Pointing out inconsistencies earned Dr. Ravnskov a reputation in medical circles as a gadfly at best and a rabble rouser at worst. His critical but scientific analysis was of little interest to the editors of the *Journal of the American Medical Association*

(*JAMA*) or the *New England Journal of Medicine* (*NEJM*), or to the mainstream medical community, which continued to advise patients to limit their intake of fats, including those foods rich in saturated fatty acids, to reduce their risk of dying from cardiovascular disease.

Stymied in his attempts to find an audience among his peers, Dr. Ravnskov put down his concerns in the book *The Cholesterol Myths,* first published in Sweden in 1991—in Swedish. The book was largely ignored and produced little impact. Even worse, critics on a Finnish TV show burned his book on the air! Several years passed, and Dr. Ravnskov thought that having *The Cholesterol Myths* published in English would jump-start the discussion. Queries to literary agents and publishers in Great Britain and the United States were summarily rejected, however.

Then the Internet arrived on the scene in the latter half of the 1990s. Suddenly Dr. Ravnskov didn't need a publisher; he posted a few chapters of *The Cholesterol Myths* on the Web, and presto, he was no longer a pariah tilting against windmills, fighting a lost cause as Don Quixote did. As word of mouth built—and people typed in "cholesterol and heart disease" in their search engines— Dr. Ravnskov received e-mails from those impressed with his measured and clear-eyed analysis, including researchers skeptical about the diet-heart connection percolating through the medical community.

One of those who corresponded with Dr. Ravnskov was Sally Fallon, a friend of mine and president of the Weston A. Price Foundation. She, too, had written an against-the-grain book on natural health called *Nourishing Traditions,* and like the Swedish doctor, she had encountered problems with finding a publisher. Sally eventually started her own publishing company, New Trends, which printed *Nourishing Traditions* and received strong sales. Because she believed in Dr. Ravnskov's message, she made *The Cholesterol Myths* one of her first acquisitions.

Dr. Ravnskov's work confirms my suspicion that the oft-recommended low-fat, high-fiber diet touted for preventing high cholesterol will never be the hoped-for panacea. Too many doctors are recommending that people stay away from certain foods that can actually be quite beneficial to overall health.

The so-called high-fat foods—steak, eggs, butter, and dairy products—when consumed from free-range and organic sources, actually contain fats that your body needs for optimal health. God, in His infinite wisdom, created fats to do the following functions: play a vital role in bone health, enhance the immune system, protect the liver from alcohol and other toxins, and guard against harmful microorganisms in the digestive tract.

The best examples of good fats are omega-3 polyunsaturated fats, monounsaturated (omega-9) fatty acids, and healthy saturated fats. Yes, you heard me right: *healthy* saturated fats. You can find these fats in a wide range of foods, including salmon, lamb, goat meat, goat's and sheep's milk, grass-fed cow's milk and cheese, coconut, flaxseed, walnuts, olives, almonds, and avocados. These fats provide us with a concentrated source of energy and are the source material for cell membranes and various hormones.

Ah, you may ask, "Didn't the Creator know that certain fatty acids are the main causes of coronary disease?"

Yes, He did, but it's the foods with *trans fat* that push up our cholesterol numbers to unacceptable levels. Trans fats are produced by heating liquid vegetable oils in the presence of hydrogen to make them solid at room temperature—a process known as hydrogenation. Food conglomerates routinely utilize hydrogenated oil in their manufacturing plants, which means that trans fats are found in nearly all our processed foods—foods that God definitely did *not* create.

I'm talking about vegetable shortening, frozen pizza, ice cream, processed cheese, potato chips, cookie dough, white bread, dinner rolls, snack foods, doughnuts, candy, salad dressing, margarine—the list is endless. Commercially prepared fried foods, like French fries and onion rings fried in polyunsaturated vegetable oils, also contain gobs of trans fat. Why do food producers employ so much chemistry? Because it allows them to produce a more competitively priced product with a longer shelf life.

Trans fat does a number on your cholesterol levels by raising your bad LDL and lowering the good HDL, which elevates the risk of heart disease as well as type 2 diabetes. Scientists have been warning us for years that eating trans fat can lead to high cholesterol and heart problems, which is why in 2006 the US Food and Drug Administration began requiring companies to state the amount of trans fat as part of the nutrition facts.

I'm convinced, however, that if you eat the foods that are part of the Great Physician's prescription for high cholesterol, you can control your cholesterol and get levels down to the healthy range.

LAYING THE GROUNDWORK

The first key—"Eat to live"—happens to be the most important prescription in *The Great Physician's Rx for High Cholesterol* because what you choose to nourish yourself with positively or negatively affects your cholesterol levels as well as your overall health. The best way to eat to live can be summed up by these two foundational principles:

1. Eat what God created for food.
2. Eat food in a form that is healthy for the body.

Eating food that God created in a form that is healthy for the body means choosing foods as close to the natural source as possible, which will provide sustenance for your body, keep your cholesterol in check, and give you the healthiest life possible. As you can probably figure out by now, I'm a proponent of natural foods grown organically, since these are foods that God created in a form healthy for the body.

The Encyclopedia of Natural Healing points out that high levels of circulating cholesterol are an attempt by the body to fight free radicals—a clear warning signal to change diet and lifestyle.[4] Free radicals are oxygen molecules with a single electron, but these unstable molecules are known to attack the immune system's cells. Antioxidants neutralize these dangerous free radicals.

The most well-known antioxidants are vitamins E and C and beta-carotene. Through scientific research, we've learned that vitamin E is a fat-soluble vitamin present in nuts, seeds, whole grains, apricots, vegetables, and eggs laid by healthy chickens. Vitamin C, chemically known as ascorbic acid, is a water-soluble vitamin present in green peppers, cabbage, spinach, broccoli, kale, cantaloupe, kiwi, strawberries, and citrus fruits and their juices. Beta-carotene is a precursor to vitamin A (which means the body converts beta-carotene to vitamin A) and is present in butter from grass-fed cows, spinach, carrots, cereal grasses such as wheat and barley, squash, broccoli, yams, tomatoes, cantaloupes, and peaches. These foods contain many other antioxidants and phytonutrient plant compounds that are being continually studied for their amazing health-giving benefits.

Take another look at the foods I just described. Do you think the average person is eating enough of these foods? Does a typical American diet of Pop-Tarts and coffee for breakfast, hamburger and fries for lunch, and spaghetti and meatballs with garlic bread for dinner fit this bill?

Optimizing nutrition begins with an awareness of what you are sending to your digestive tract. To begin with, everything you put into your mouth is a protein, a fat, or a carbohydrate. Let's take a closer look at these macronutrients.

THE FIRST WORD ON PROTEINS

Proteins, one of the basic components of foods, are the essential building blocks of the body and involved in the function of every living cell, just like cholesterol. One of protein's main functions is to provide specific nutrient material to grow and repair cells.

All proteins are combinations of twenty-two amino acids, which build and maintain the body's organs, including the heart, as well as the muscles and nerves, to name a few important duties. Your body, however, cannot produce all twenty-two amino acids that you need to live a robust life. Scientists have discovered that eight essential amino acids are missing, meaning that they must come from sources outside the body. I know the following fact drives vegetarians and vegans crazy, but animal protein—chicken, beef, lamb, dairy, eggs, and so forth—is the *only* complete protein source providing the Big Eight amino acids in the right quantities and ratios.

I don't believe that you have to give up red meat when you have high cholesterol *if* you're served the leanest, healthiest sources of animal protein available, which come from organically raised cattle, sheep, goats, buffalo, and venison—animals that graze on pastureland grasses. Lean red meat from grass-fed anmals is lower in calories and doesn't contain as much fat as grain-fed beef.

Everyone agrees that chicken and fish are excellent sources of protein for those with high cholesterol. I'm a huge fan of free-range chicken and fish captured from lakes, streambeds, or ocean depths. Fish with scales and fins, caught in the wild, contain healthy fats, vitamins, and minerals, and provide all the essential amino acids. Wild fish, which is nutritionally far superior to farm-raised, should be consumed liberally, whether you have high cholesterol or not.

A REPRISE ON FATS

The problem with the standard American diet is that people eat too many of the wrong foods containing the wrong fats and not enough of the right foods with the right fats. On top of that, there's a lot of confusion about cholesterol and fats in this world because we hear how bad they are when, in fact, cholesterol and fats are essential because they regulate insulin levels and trigger enzymes that convert food into energy.

Eating healthy fats can have a protective effect against heart disease. I'm referring to foods loaded with the following:

- omega-3 fatty acids

- monounsaturated (omega-9) fatty acids

- conjugated linoleic acid (CLA)

- key omega-6 fats, such as gamma-linolenic acid (GLA)

- healthy saturated fatty acids such as short- and medium-chain fatty acids; for example, organic butter and unrefined coconut and palm oils

It bears noting again that these good fats are found in a wide range of foods including: salmon, cod-liver oil, lamb and goat meat, high omega-3 eggs, dairy products derived from goat's milk, sheep's milk, cow's milk and butter from grass-fed animals, flax-seeds, walnuts, olives, macadamia nuts, and avocados.

You may have noticed that I haven't said anything about cutting eggs from your diet, although I'm sure you've heard public health advocates declare that individuals with high cholesterol should avoid consuming eggs. Their nutritional logic travels along these lines:

1. High cholesterol levels are bad for the heart.
2. Eating foods high in cholesterol raises cholesterol levels in the blood.
3. Eggs are high in cholesterol (213 mg per egg).
4. Therefore, eggs are bad for your cholesterol levels, so don't eat eggs.

I beg to differ, and so do others I respect. Michael Murray, the primary author of *The Encyclopedia of Healing Foods*, said that several recent studies have indicated that moderate egg consumption has little effect on cholesterol levels.[5] In a study of more than eighty thousand female nurses, Harvard University researchers actually found that *increasing* cholesterol intake by 200 mg for every 1,000 calories in the diet (about an egg a day) did not appreciably increase the risk for heart disease.[6]

Other health experts have been wising up to the benefits of the egg, which is a nutrient-dense food that packs six grams of protein, a bit of vitamin B_{12}, vitamin E, lutein, riboflavin, folic acid, calcium, zinc, iron, and essential fatty acids into a mere seventy-five calories. As long as you're shopping for certified organic, high omega-3 eggs, you'll be eating one of the healthiest foods out there.

As for cooking with oil, the top two on my list are extra virgin coconut oil and extra virgin olive oil, which are beneficial to the body and aid metabolism. I urge you to cook with extra virgin coconut oil, which is an extremely healthy food that far too few people consume.

GO FOR THOSE CARBS

By definition, carbohydrates are the starches and sugars produced by plant foods, and they are carried in the blood as glucose and regulated by insulin, a hormone that holds the key to each cell's nutritional door. Thanks to the low-carb diet popularized by two cardiologists—Dr. Robert Atkins and Dr. Arthur Agatston, creators of the Atkins diet and the South Beach Diet, respectively—Americans have been on a carbohydrate witch hunt for the last decade or so.

The Atkins diet, to single out the oldest and most widely practiced low-carb diet, calls for a high consumption of conventionally raised and processed meats (ham, bacon, pepperoni, salami, and hot dogs) that are high in unhealthy fats, which can only increase your risk of a heart attack while driving up your cholesterol levels. The Atkins diet also forbids plentiful amounts of fruits and high-starch vegetables, which are loaded with fiber and antioxidants and are part of the Great Physician's prescription for high cholesterol.

How does one reconcile that nutritional advice with the American Heart Association's recommendation that we eat at least five servings of fruits and vegetables daily to significantly reduce three of the major risk factors for a heart attack—high blood cholesterol, high blood pressure, and excess body weight?

I don't believe that curbing your carbs will rein in high cholesterol anyway. Instead, you should add unrefined carbohydrates including the aforementioned fruits and veggies as well as
whole grains such as oats, wheat, rye, corn, rice, and barley to
your diet. Whole grain foods contain all the nutrition found in
the whole grains, including the bran and the germ, so they're
higher in fiber and the healthy fatty acids.

One of the best unrefined carbohydrates for maintaining
healthy cholesterol levels and a healthy heart is whole oats, which
contains beta-glucans from soluble fiber. Soluble fiber does not dis-
solve in water and binds cholesterol as it wends its way through the
digestive tract. Oat bran is an excellent source of soluble fiber, and
Prescription for Natural Cures points to twenty studies showing that
oat bran reduces total and LDL cholesterol when consumed on a
daily basis. "One bowl of oatmeal can lower cholesterol levels
between 8 and 23 percent in just three weeks," stated *Prescription
for Natural Cures.*[7]

The U.S. Food and Drug Administration concluded that
there is a link between the soluble fiber in whole-oat foods and a
reduction in coronary heart disease risk because the beta-glucans
in soluble fiber is the primary component responsible for lowering the bad LDL cholesterol levels.[8] That's why you're seeing a lot
more red hearts on cereal boxes like Quaker Oats oatmeal and
Kashi Heart to Heart cereal. Products with beta-glucans from oat
soluble fiber qualify for the American Heart Association's "Heart
Healthy" seal of approval and can legally print the following
health claim—approved by the FDA—on the outside of the
package: "Soluble fiber from [insert your product's brand name],

in a diet low in saturated fat and cholesterol, may reduce the risk of coronary heart disease and lower blood cholesterol."

Unfortunately some oatmeal and much of the cereal—and bread—in this country are made from wheat and other grains subjected to a refining process, which is then enriched with certain nutrients removed during the refining process. The only thing enriched flour enriches is the bad LDL cholesterol levels, perhaps triglycerides in the blood, and, of course, insulin levels, which is why foods made with white, unbleached, or enriched flour should be avoided completely.

Instead, buy organic flour with the words *stone ground* or *whole grain* on the label, or shop for breads with the words *yeast free* or *sprouted* on the package label. These whole grain products—along with old-fashioned oatmeal—haven't been stripped of their vital fiber, vitamin, and mineral components. The Harvard School of Public Health analyzed diet and health records of more than twenty-seven-thousand men ages forty to seventy-five over a period of fourteen years and found that those eating the most whole grains cut their heart disease risk by almost 20 percent.[9]

Eating unrefined carbohydrate foods also introduces fiber into your body. Fiber is the indigestible remnant of plant cells found in vegetables, fruits, whole grains, nuts, seeds, and beans. Fiber-rich foods take longer to break down and are partially indigestible, which means that as these foods work their way through the digestive tract, they absorb water and increase the elimination of waste matter in the large intestine. Fiber also attracts and eliminates excess fat from the body.

Good sources of fiber are berries, fruits with edible skins

(apples, pears, and grapes), citrus fruits, and whole grains like quinoa, millet, amaranth, buckwheat, and brown rice. (I especially like gluten-free whole grains.) You'll do just fine with eating green peas, carrots, cucumbers, zucchini, tomatoes, and baked or boiled unpeeled potatoes. Green leafy vegetables such as spinach are also fiber-rich.

Eating foods high in fiber will immediately improve your blood sugar levels by slowing the absorption of sugars into your bloodstream. A diet high in fiber can reduce a woman's risk of coronary heart disease up to 23 percent, according to a study released in the *Journal of the American Medical Association*. After controlling for various factors, researchers found that women who consumed the most fiber each day, around twenty-three grams, reduced their risk of coronary heart disease.[10]

The Top Healing Foods

Just as a diet heavy in junk foods is a primary cause of high cholesterol, making changes in your diet is a great way to fight it. I've been talking in general terms about nutritional recommendations, but now I would like to be more specific. Before doing that, however, let me remind you to chew your food well. If people tease you about "inhaling" your food, then you're eating too fast. I recommend chewing each mouthful of food twenty-five to seventy-five times before swallowing. This advice may sound ridiculous, but I know that a conscious effort to chew food slowly ensures that plenty of digestive juices are added to the food as it begins to wind through the digestive tract.

Got enough to chew on? Excellent. Let's take a closer look at what you should and shouldn't be eating when it comes to trying to lower cholesterol:

1. Healthy animal foods. I've already made a strong case for eating meat from organically raised cattle, sheep, goats, buffalo, and venison that graze on nature's bountiful grasses as well as fish caught in the wild. For those with high cholesterol, the healthiest meat is fish caught in the wild, including salmon, sardines, herring, mackerel, tuna, snapper, bass, and cod. Wild-caught fish are a rich source of omega-3 fatty acids, which are also good for heart health.

One of the first associations between omega-3 fatty acids and human health happened in the 1970s during a study of the Inuit people of Greenland. Scientists discovered that Inuits suffered far less coronary heart disease than Europeans, even though their diet was off-the-chart high in fat from eating whales and seals—including their blubber—as well as copious amounts of salmon.[11]

2. Cultured dairy products from goats, cows, and sheep. Medical doctors lump the saturated fats in dairy products in the same category as red meat, implicating the fat intake as a key factor behind high cholesterol and cardiovascular disease. Thus, doctors recommend that we should not eat full-fat dairy products. When reaching for a gallon of milk at the supermarket, they say, be sure to choose a low-fat version like 2 percent or skim.

I don't see things the same way, because I have never heard

of a milking cow or goat that could produce 2 percent or skim milk. Reduced-fat milk is less nutritious, less digestible, and can cause allergies. When it comes to keeping cholesterol levels in check, I recommend that you purchase dairy products derived from goat's milk and sheep's milk rather than cow's milk, although dairy products from organic or grass-fed cows can be excellent as well. The reason I prefer goat's milk and goat's cheese lies in the structure of the goat's milk: its fat and protein molecules are tiny in size, which allows for rapid absorption in the digestive tract. Milk fat from healthy milk (organic, grass-fed) also contains a number of bioactive components, including conjugated linoleic acid (CLA). "Conjugated linoleic acid has been shown to possess activities that prevent cancer and the formation of cholesterol-containing plaques that contribute to heart disease [and high cholesterol]," said Michael Murray, author of *The Encyclopedia of Healing Foods*.[12]

Goat's milk is less allergenic because it does not contain the same complex proteins found in cow's milk. I also recommend you consume milk in its cultured or fermented form such as yogurt and kefir. The fermentation process makes the milk easier to digest, and its nutrients are more usable by the body. Cultured or fermented dairy products contain beneficial microorganisms or probiotics that help maintain healthy cholesterol levels and even lower elevated levels.

There's another bit of pertinent information regarding dairy products and heart health. Commercial milk these days, for the most part, is pasteurized and homogenized, but it wasn't always so. Up until the start of the twentieth century, people drank milk straight from cows and goats. "Sure, it was contaminated, but so was everything else," wrote William Campbell Douglass II, M.D. and author of *The Milk Book: The Milk of Human Kindness Is Not Pasteurized.* When milk was bottled for sale and consumption, globules of butterfat separated from the milk and floated to the top of the bottle, which is where we received the expression: "The cream always rises to the top."

Milk producers thought that milk separated into cream and skim milk was unappetizing for consumers. Auguste Gaulin, a Frenchman, patented a nifty machine in 1899 that shot milk through a fine nozzle to break up the fat globules so that the butterfat would not rise to the top. This process became known as homogenization, but it didn't become popular until the 1930s.

Researchers have learned that the homogenization process creates an enzyme called xanthine oxidase, or XO, which contributes to heart disease by damaging the arteries and building up arterial plaque. "A substantial body of evidence has accumulated to suggest a role for the xanthine oxidase metabolic pathway [otherwise known as XO] in the pathophysiology of chronic heart failure and other cardiovascular diseases," according to German medical researchers Wolfram Doehner and S. D. Anker.[13] The milk industry says that pasteurization kills XO, but according to Dr. Douglass, 40 percent of XO is left in an active state.

I've been heavily influenced by reading Dr. Douglass's book, which makes a strong case for drinking certified raw milk instead of homogenized, pasteurized milk that fills the refrigerated cases of supermarkets. Unfortunately, certified raw milk is not widely available, thanks to the "Got Milk?" lobby and the National Dairy Council. If you can't find certified raw milk, cultured or fermented dairy such as yogurt and kefir is the next best thing. If you do buy fluid milk, make sure that you consume pasteurized but nonhomogenized milk, which is usually sold in glass bottles at the health food store. Goat's milk is usually a superior option because goat's milk is naturally homogenized and therefore does not contain XO.

3. Fruits and vegetables. When it comes to cholesterol, you'll never go wrong reaching for an apple or making yourself a salad for lunch. Nearly five thousand participants in the National Heart, Lung, and Blood Institute's Family Heart Study consumed, on average, a shade over three servings of fruits and veggies a day. (Three servings a day match what the average American eats in fruits and vegetables on a daily basis.) In the study, men and women with the highest daily consumption—more than four servings a day—had significantly lower levels of bad LDL cholesterol than those with lower consumption.[14] Thus, increasing your consumption of fruits and vegetables by just one serving a day can have a real impact on cholesterol levels.

Soluble fiber in fruits and vegetables is thought to block the absorption of cholesterol from food. Pears, apples, grapes, grapefruit, bananas, and oranges contain high levels of pectin, a natural fiber known for lowering cholesterol. Don't peel the skin off pears, apples, or grapes because that's where the most pectin lies. Blueberries make another great snack. In addition to the soluble fiber, these fruits are loaded with antioxidants that fight free radicals and have been shown to improve cholesterol levels. Eat your fruits fresh off the farm because whole fruits contain more pectin than fruit juices.

If you're looking to get a handle on cholesterol, you won't go wrong making a stir-fry of vegetables—with liberal amounts of garlic and onions, of course. Besides being cholesterol-free, most vegetables are low-glycemic, high-fiber foods that can be broken down by the body into simple sugars. Green leafy vegetables such as lettuce, spinach, and Swiss chard and cruciferous vegetables such as broccoli, cauliflower, cabbage, Brussels sprouts, and kale can have a real impact on cholesterol levels.

4. Avocados, garlic, and onions. No, I'm not just talking about some ingredients you can use to make homemade guacamole. Each of these cholesterol-free ingredients is worth munching on or mixing into your meals. An avocado has five grams of mono-unsaturated fat—a type of fat that helps raise levels of good HDL cholesterol while lowering bad LDL cholesterol—and is loaded with fiber and vitamin E. And you can pass the chips with this last bit of news: avocados pack more of the cholesterol-smashing beta-sitosterol—a beneficial plant-based fat—than any other fruit.[15]

Garlic may lower cholesterol as well, which means you may have to bear some bad breath to enjoy the benefit of this pungent herb. The jury is still out on garlic, however. Researchers at the University of Essex in England examined the findings of thirteen different studies on the link between garlic and cholesterol and found mixed results: some showed that garlic reduced cholesterol while others noted that garlic was not an efficient way to decrease total cholesterol levels.[16]

Garlic has exhibited a wide spectrum of beneficial effects, so I lean toward studies that demonstrated its ability to lower cholesterol levels. Be sure to use fresh garlic in your foods or supplement with an aged garlic extract.

As for onions, the *Encyclopedia of Natural Medicine* reports that a study in India found that those who consumed fifty grams of garlic and six hundred grams of onions (more than a pound!) experienced considerably lower cholesterol and triglyceride counts than those who ate a small amount of garlic and onions or none at all.[17] But at least they had no problems getting dates.

I'm confident that garlic and onions are worthwhile foods to eat when you're dealing with cholesterol. Please note that I liberally include the addition of garlic and onions to my suggested meals in the Great Physician's Rx for High Cholesterol Battle Plan found on page 76.

5. Nuts, seeds, and raw trail mix. Remember that one of the first things physicians forbid to someone with high cholesterol levels is eating nuts. That advice is nuts, and here's why. As Ron Rosedale, M.D., reported in his excellent book, *The Rosedale Diet,* study after study began appearing in medical journals noting that people who eat nuts have a lower incidence of heart disease and are generally healthier than those who don't eat nuts. "Nut critics are now eating their words," Dr. Rosedale wrote. "The FDA recently approved nuts for the healthy claim to be used on package labels. The claim states, 'Scientific evidence suggests but does not prove that eating 1.5 ounces per day of most nuts, as part of a diet low in saturated fat and cholesterol, may reduce the risk of heart disease.'"[18]

What are the best nuts to eat? Walnuts, almonds, macadamia nuts, and flaxseeds would be the best nuts and seeds to munch on. Better yet, a certified organic raw trail mix is a delicious, nutrient-dense superfood packed with all the right vitamins, minerals, essential fatty oils, and antioxidants. You can find a recipe for a healthy trail mix by visiting www.BiblicalHealthInstitute.com.

6. Cacao. Cacao—the purest and original chocolate—is an excellent source of antioxidants, fatty acids, and other valuable trace minerals. Raw cacao, which is the base ingredient of chocolate, has ten times more antioxidants than blueberries, twenty times more than red wine, and thirty times more than green tea. You can find recommendations for my favorite cacao chocolate snack by visiting www.BiblicalHealthInstitute.com and clicking on the Resource Guide.

7. Old-fashioned oatmeal. I've already mentioned how oatmeal can lower cholesterol levels, and the beta-glucans found in oats is the primary component responsible for lowering the bad LDL cholesterol levels. Although oatmeal involves some preparation time in the morning, your cholesterol count will thank you for making the effort. Purchase only oatmeal from organic sources.

8. Water. F. Batmanghelidj, M.D., and author of *Your Body's Many Cries for Water,* contends that increased cholesterol production in the body is a direct consequence of chronic dehydration. "Raised cholesterol is a sign that the cells of the body have developed a defense mechanism against the stronger osmotic forces of blood," Dr. Batmanghelidj wrote. "Cholesterol is the natural sort of waterproof clay that, when poured in the gaps of the cell membrane, helps keep the membrane's architecture intact and prevents excess water loss. In chronic dehydration, additional amounts of cholesterol will be produced by the liver cells and poured into the circulation for the common use of all cells."[19]

Dr. Batmanghelidj recommends drinking an ample amount of water a half hour before eating. By this action, the cells will become well hydrated when it is time to begin the digestion process and won't need to tap into water held inside the cells lining the blood vessels.

You should drink a minimum of eight glasses of water a day to stay hydrated. Drinking plenty of water is not only healthy for the body, but it may save your life. Sure, you'll go to the bathroom more often, but is that so bad? Drinking plenty of water is not only healthy for the body, but it's a key part of the Great Physician's Rx for High Cholesterol Battle Plan, so keep a water bottle close by and drink water before, during, and in between meals.

9. Green tea. Made from unfermented leaves and containing very high concentrations of antioxidants, green tea has demonstrated an ability to lower total cholesterol and raise good HDL cholesterol levels. The University of Maryland Medical Center reported the results of one animal study suggesting that the polyphenols in green tea may block the intestinal absorption of cholesterol and promote its excretion from the body.[20]

10. Organic whole food bars, whole food meal or shake, or fruit powder with beta-glucans. Soluble fiber is an active agent for reducing blood cholesterol, and these three foods and snacks have a component of soluble fiber known as beta-glucans. Adding beta-glucans to the diet can reduce cholesterol levels by nearly 10 percent, according to a landmark study conducted at Ottawa Civic Hospital by the University of Ottawa.[21] You'll find recommendations on how to include these healthy foods and snacks into your diet in the Battle Plan.

WHAT NOT TO EAT: "THE DIRTY DOZEN"

No matter where your cholesterol levels are, the following foods—which I call "The Dirty Dozen"—should never find a way onto your plate or into your hands. Some I've already discussed elsewhere in this chapter, while the rest are presented here with a short commentary:

1. Processed meat and pork products. These meats top my list because they are staples in the standard American diet and are extremely unhealthy. You must steer clear of breakfast links, bacon, lunchmeats, ham, bratwurst, and other sausages because they introduce toxins into the bloodstream. These processed meats, which are high in unhealthy fats, contain additives like nitrates that were introduced during the curing process. Nitrates can convert into nitrite, which can form into nitrosamines, a powerful cancer-causing chemical.

Many processed meats—including pepperoni, salami, and hot dogs—are made from pork products. In all of my previous books, I've consistently pointed out that pork—America's "other white meat"—should be avoided because pigs were called "unclean" and "detestable" in Leviticus and Exodus. God created pigs as scavengers—animals that survive just fine on any farm slop or water swill tossed their way. Pigs have a simple stomach arrangement: whatever a pig eats goes down the hatch, straight into the stomach, and out the back door in four hours max. They'll even eat their own excrement, if hungry enough.

Even if you decide to keep eating commercial beef instead of the organic version, I absolutely urge you to stop eating pork. Read Leviticus 11 and Deuteronomy 14 to learn what God said about eating clean versus unclean animals, where Hebrew words used to describe "unclean meats" can be translated as "foul" and "putrid," the same terms the Bible uses to describe human waste.

Eating unclean foods fouls the body and may lead to increases in heart disease and cancer by introducing toxins into the bloodstream. God declared these meats detestable because He understands the ramifications of eating them, and you should as well.

2. Shellfish and fish without fins and scales, such as catfish, shark, and eel. Shellfish and fish without fins and scales, such as catfish, shark, and eel, are also described in Leviticus 11 and Deuteronomy 14 as "unclean meats." God called hard-shelled crustaceans such as lobster, crabs, shrimp, and clams unclean because they are "bottom feeders," content to sustain themselves on excrement from other fish. To be sure, this purifies water but does nothing for the health of their flesh—or yours, if you eat them.

Am I saying au revoir, sayonara, and adios to lobster thermidor, shrimp tempura, and carnitas burritos? You can bet your scampi.

3. Hydrogenated oils. For many years, food manufacturers have produced margarine by employing a process called hydrogenation in which liquid vegetable oil is injected with hydrogen gas at high temperatures under high pressure to make margarine easy to spread. The problem with hydrogenation is that it spawns trans fats by the truckload, making margarine or any type of hydrogenated oil—soybean, safflower, cottonseed, or corn—terribly unhealthy for the body.

Now that the public is listening up to the dangers of trans fats, food manufacturers have gone back into the laboratory to see if they could come up with a formula to make margarine from nonhydrogenated sources. Here's what their chemists found: instead of hydrogenating liquid vegetable oil, food manufacturers could add a dabble of modified palm and palm kernel oil to keep their soft margarine trans-fat free. That's exactly what they've done, which is why you have seen those heavily advertised spreads that "promote healthy cholesterol levels." I'm talking about soft-tub brands like Take Control, Benecol, and Promise.

Sorry, but low-cholesterol margarine is definitely not a food that God created. "It's ironic and unfortunate that margarine and even vegetable shortening are touted as heart-healthy products," say the authors of *Prescription for Natural Cures*. "For years, doctors have told us to replace butter with margarine . . . but as you probably heard, researchers have discovered that the hydrogenation process produces altered molecules called trans-fatty acids. These substances appear to pack a double whammy: not only do they raise LDL, they lower HDL and cause free radical damage."[22]

Commercial cakes, pastries, desserts, and just about every food sold in a gas station convenience store are made with hydrogenated or partially hydrogenated fats.

4. Artificial sweeteners. Aspartame (found in NutraSweet and Equal), saccharin (Sweet 'N Low), and sucralose (Splenda)—nocholesterol chemicals several hundred times sweeter than sugar—should be completely avoided whether they come in blue, pink, or yellow packets. Simply put, in my opinion, these are not foods at all, but combinations of artificial chemicals that may lead to serious problems for those who consume them.

5. White flour. White flour isn't a chemical like artificial sweeteners, but it's virtually worthless from a nutritional standpoint and can stimulate the body to produce excess cholesterol.

6. White sugar. Sugar, along with alcohol found in wine, beer, and spirits, stimulates the liver to produce more cholesterol. If you have a cholesterol problem, stay away from alcoholic drinks, and you shouldn't be eating sweets or desserts loaded with sugar anyway.

7. Soft drinks. Nothing more than liquefied sugar. A twenty-ounce cola drink is the equivalent of eating fifteen teaspoons of sugar. Diet drinks loaded with artificial sweeteners are even worse.

8. Corn syrup. Another version of sugar and just as bad for you, if not worse.

9. Pasteurized homogenized skim milk. As I said, whole organic, nonhomogenized milk is better, and goat's milk is best.

10. Hydrolyzed soy protein. Hydrolyzed soy protein is found in imitation meat products such as imitation crab. I would look at hydrolyzed soy protein like I would regard meat cured with nitrites: stay away from it. You're always going to be better off eating organic meats.

Since we're talking about soy, you'll hear that various soy products, such as soy milk and tofu, are recommended for their low-cholesterol qualities. Yet the American Heart Association, in a study of a decade of studies on the healthy benefits of soy, concluded that soy-based foods don't significantly lower cholesterol.

Another organization that I respect, the Weston A. Price Foundation, noted that soy proponents claim that soy helps the heart because it lowers cholesterol, but no studies have proven that soy can prevent heart disease.[23]

11. Artificial flavors and colors. These are never good for you under the best of circumstances, and certainly not when you're battling high cholesterol.

12. Anything fried in unhealthy oils. Fried foods and cholesterol go together like . . . cheeseburgers topped with bacon.

EAT: WHAT FOODS ARE EXTRAORDINARY, AVERAGE, OR TROUBLE?

I've prepared a comprehensive list of foods that are ranked in descending order based on their health-giving qualities. Foods at the top of the list are healthier than those at the bottom. The best foods to serve and eat are what I call "Extraordinary," which God created for us to eat and will give you the best chance to live a long and happy life. If you are battling high cholesterol, however, it's best to consume foods from the Extraordinary category more than 75 percent of the time.

Foods in the Average category should make up less than 25 percent of your daily diet. If you need to lower your cholesterol levels, these foods should be consumed sparingly.

Foods in the Trouble category should be consumed with extreme caution. If your doctor has put you on notice that you have high cholesterol, you should avoid these foods completely.

For a complete listing of Extraordinary, Average, and Trouble foods, visit www.BiblicalHealthInstitute.com/EAT.

> ### *Practice Fasting Once a Week*
>
> I'm a firm believer in the value of giving the body's digestive system time off from the round-the-clock digestive cycle, which will also give your heart and your

liver less work to do—good news for those battling high cholesterol.

I think it's better—and more realistic—to concentrate on completing a one-day partial fast once a week. Fasting is a form of discipline that isn't easy for someone who's never done it. If you've never voluntarily fasted for a day, I urge you to try it—preferably toward the end of the week. I've found that Thursdays or Fridays work best for me because the week is winding down and the weekend is coming up. For instance, I won't eat breakfast and lunch so that when I break my fast and eat dinner that night, my body has gone between eighteen and twenty hours without food since I last ate dinner the night before.

The benefits are immediate: you'll feel great, lose weight, look younger, save money, save time, and become closer to the Lord. Fasting is a means of denying the flesh because the stomach and the brain work overtime in reminding you "Hey! I'm hungry!" That's why they call it the fasting headache. When you fast and pray (two words that seem to go hand in hand in Scripture), you are pursuing God in your life and opening yourself to experiencing a renewed sense of well-being and dependence upon the Lord.

℞ THE GREAT PHYSICIAN'S RX FOR HIGH CHOLESTEROL: EAT TO LIVE

- *Eat only foods God created.*

- *Eat foods in a form that is healthy for the body.*

- *Increase consumption of fruits, vegetables, grains, and cereals, which do not contain cholesterol.*

- *Avoid foods containing hydrogenated oils.*

- *Consume lean meats from organically raised cattle as well as wild-caught fish high in omega-3 fatty acids.*

- *Snack on trail mix and raw nuts and seeds.*

- *Consume whole oats in cereals, bars, and shakes, which contain beta-glucans from soluble fiber.*

- *Practice fasting one day per week.*

- *Drink eight or more glasses of pure water per day as well as green tea.*

Take Action

To learn how to incorporate the principles of eating to live into your daily lifestyle, please turn to page 76 for the Great Physician's Rx for High Cholesterol Battle Plan.

KEY #2

Supplement Your Diet with Whole Food Nutritionals, Living Nutrients, and Superfoods

When Carol Wootten's doctor penned a prescription for Niaspan, he was asking her to take a prolonged-release drug that contained a B-complex vitamin known as niacin.

Niacin is found naturally in meat (especially red meat), poultry, fish, legumes, and yeast, and is also present in cereal grains such as corn and wheat. This member of the B-vitamin family is known for its role in energy metabolism for cells and repair of DNA. When niacin is formulated into a cholesterol-lowering supplement, it is derived from nicotinic acid, which was first discovered when chemists experimented with the oxidation of nicotine.

Yes, you read right: nicotine . . . the addictive portion of tobacco products. When this oxidized version of nicotinic acid was realized, men and women in science thought it would be prudent to choose a generic name to dissociate it from nicotine and to avoid the idea that smoking provided vitamins or that wholesome foods such as salmon, tuna, poultry, peanuts, sunflower seeds, and legumes—which all naturally have niacin—contained a poison. So the name *niacin* was derived from *ni*cotinic *ac*id + vitam*in*.[1]

Researchers began testing niacin synthesized from nicotinic acid in the 1950s, and studies over the years have generally verified that niacin lowers total cholesterol as well LDL cholesterol

37

and triglycerides while raising HDL cholesterol levels. Yet as Carol Wootten learned to her chagrin, the chemical properties of niacin that were part of her Niaspan prescription subjected her to the bothersome side effects of flushing—red skin resembling a sunburn, itching, and tingling sensations.

You may be thinking that niacin, since it's part of the B-complex family, would be part of the Great Physician's Rx for High Cholesterol Battle Plan, but that's not the case. I do not generally recommend taking isolated nutrients such as niacin since isolated nutrients sometimes work like prescription drugs with attendant side effects. "Large doses of niacin are not supplements, but drugs," stated Louis Lasagna, dean of the Sackler School of Graduate Biomedical Sciences at Tufts University in Boston. "Niacin is capable of damaging the liver, activating peptic ulcers, impairing glucose tolerance, and precipitating gouty attacks."[2]

While I believe niacin can be effective if used correctly, I prefer a different approach when it comes to supplementing your diet to improve cholesterol levels, the second key that will unlock your health potential.

From the outset, though, please know that I'm not one who believes high cholesterol can be turned around with a bottle of pills. After years of study in naturopathic medicine and nutrition, I understand better than most that dietary supplements are just what they say they are—supplements, not a substitute to make up for an inadequate diet and unhealthy lifestyle.

The nutritional supplement highest on my list is high omega-3 cod-liver oil. Remember how I talked in the last chapter about eating wild-caught fish because of its high omega-3 fatty acid content? These marvelous oils extracted from the filleted livers of cold-water cod harvested from icy North Atlantic waters contain off-the-chart amounts of omega-3 fatty acids, vitamin A, and vitamin D—nutrients difficult to obtain from our modern diets.

High omega-3 cod-liver oil is brimming with more vitamin A and vitamin D per unit of weight than other common food. A tablespoon of cod-liver oil (about 15 grams) contains 15,000 IU of vitamin A (almost three times more than beef liver, the next richest source), and 1,500 IU of vitamin D (almost four times more than lard, the next richest source).[3]

Another thing in cod-liver oil's favor is that the omega-3 fatty acids are anti-inflammatory, where other fatty acids are known to induce inflammation in the body. Arachidonic acid—an unsaturated fatty acid found in meat and dairy products—dominates the average diet in this country. Without the high omega-3 fatty acids found in foods and supplements such as omega-3 cod-liver oil to balance things, your body's health would be tipped in favor of inflammation and constriction of the blood vessels. Not good if you're fighting high cholesterol.

Some people turn up their noses to cod-liver oil and call it an acquired taste, but after a decade of sipping spoonfuls of this golden oil, I'm at the point where I can drink the stuff right out of the bottle. If you can't stomach the thought of taking omega-3 cod-liver oil by the teaspoon, you can now take this important nutrient in easy-to-swallow liquid capsules. (For recommended brands, visit www.BiblicalHealthInstitute.com and click on the Resource Guide.)

The next item on the Great Physician's supplement protocol

would be a whole food multivitamin containing different compounds such as minerals, organic acids, antioxidants, and key vitamins. Whole food multivitamins are more costly to produce since the ingredients—fruits, vegetables, sea vegetables, seeds, spices, vitamins and minerals, and so forth—are put through a fermentation process similar to the digestive process of the body, but they are well worth the extra money. They contain high levels of vitamins E and C, antioxidants that help fight high cholesterol. Vitamin E protects and maintains cellular membranes while vitamin C promotes healthy cell development and helps protect against heart disease.

You should consider increasing your intake of antioxidants and polyphenolics (plant compounds that provide much of the flavor, color, and taste to fruits and vegetables) by seeking out grape and pomegranate extracts, which have cholesterol-lowering properties. A recent University of California at Davis human clinical trial conducted by cardiovascular researchers demonstrated that those taking three hundred milligrams of grape seed extract reduced their bad LDL cholesterol levels.[4] As for pomegranates, an Israeli study conducted at the Rambam Medical Center in Haifa noted that pomegranate polyphenols could protect the body against LDL formation.[5]

Beverage extracts should not be overlooked either. Tea, the second most consumed beverage in the world, has long been thought to lower cholesterol, but even researchers at Vanderbilt University Medical Center were surprised by the first human study testing a green tea extract. Participants in the 2003 study experienced a 16 percent reduction in their LDL cholesterol levels.[6] White tea, which is produced from immature tea leaves just before the buds have fully opened, contains more polyphenols (and less caffeine) than any other type of tea, and thus is believed to have cholesterol-lowering properties.

Besides these teas, there are a pair of adaptogenic herbs that help control cholesterol levels: the eastern Indian herb *ashwaghandha* and the Russian herb *Rhodiola rosea,* when mixed into hot water like tea or taken as extracts in high-quality supplements, revitalize metabolic processes and support cholesterol levels. Another substance similar to tea, *yerba maté,* is a beverage made from the leaves and stems of trees native to the rainforests of Paraguay, Brazil, and Argentina. Like green and white tea, yerba maté is high in antioxidants and polyphenols.

EAT YOUR GREEN FOODS

In Key #1 of *The Great Physician's Rx for High Cholesterol,* I mentioned the importance of eating green leafy vegetables for their cholesterol-fighting qualities. High in fiber, brimming with antioxidants, and excellent fuel for healthy cells, leafy greens and assorted vegetables are some of the best cholesterol-fighting foods out there.

If only Americans ate their veggies.

Does that sound like you? Were salad bowls and vegetable dishes mere table decorations to your meat and potatoes? Did your parents incessantly nag you to finish your green beans or eat your salad before you could dig into dessert?

If you *hated* vegetables growing up, or are a reluctant adult who manages a few forkfuls at mealtime, then consider taking a green food supplement that is a certified organic blend of dried green vegetables, fermented vegetables, sea vegetables, micro-algaes such as spirulina and chlorella, and sprouted grains and seeds. When you drink or swallow green foods, your body is taking in one of the most nutrient-dense foods on this green earth. I recommend the consumption of green superfood powders and caplets. All you do is mix the powder in water or your favorite juice or swallow a handful of caplets.

You should also look into a whole food fiber blend with flaxseeds and soluble fiber from oats, both of which help move your cholesterol numbers in the right direction. Remember, fiber lowers bad LDL cholesterol levels and improves regularity, which helps to efficiently eliminate toxins from the body. Since most of us receive about one-fifth of the optimal amount of fiber in our daily diet, I recommend taking a whole food fiber supplement. Look for one with beta-glucans from oat soluble fiber because of its ability to reduce serum levels of cholesterol, triglycerides, and blood glucose. Whole food fiber mix with beta-glucans can be added to a morning smoothie.

When searching for a fiber product that's right for you, be sure to choose a brand made from organic seeds, grains, and legumes that are fermented or sprouted for ease of digestion. I highly recommend taking both a green food and a whole food fiber blend that contain an oat-based product rich in beta-glucans soluble fiber, an ingredient in a variety of cereals and food bars. Beta-glucans from soluble oat fiber is a functional food that can be mixed into juice drinks, smoothies, dairy products, soups, and sauces. Best of all, this all-natural product is manufactured 100 percent organically. (For recommended

brands, visit www.BiblicalHealthInstitute.com and click on the
Resource Guide.)

R✗ THE GREAT PHYSICIAN'S RX FOR HIGH CHOLESTEROL: SUPPLEMENT YOUR DIET WITH WHOLE FOOD NUTRITIONALS, LIVING NUTRIENTS, AND SUPERFOODS

- *Consume one to three teaspoons or three to nine capsules of omega-3 cod-liver oil per day.*

- *Take a whole food living multivitamin with each meal.*

- *Take a green food and whole food fiber blend with beta-glucans from soluble oat fiber twice per day, morning and evening.*

Take Action

To learn how to incorporate the principles of supplementing your diet with whole food nutritionals, living nutrients, and superfoods into your daily regimen, please turn to page 76 for the Great Physician's Rx for High Cholesterol Battle Plan.

KEY #3

Practice Advanced Hygiene

I will be the first to admit that dipping your face into a basin of facial solution, cleaning under your fingernails with a special soap, or washing your hands after going to the bathroom doesn't sound as if it has much to do with high cholesterol. But there's an aspect to good hygiene that's relevant to this discussion, and it has to do with how the body produces cholesterol to seal up cracks in the arteries that may have been caused by oxidative stress and/or inflammation, which could be caused by bad germs, toxins, or allergens attacking the body.

First, a little high school biology lesson.

Every day of your life, your body wards off gazillions of germs, which break down your immune system and make you more susceptible to health problems. Every *other* day of your life (or so it seems), little "ow-ees" happen: a badly stubbed toe, a mosquito bite, a slight sunburn, a pulled muscle, or a nick while shaving your legs (for you gals) or your face and neck (for you guys). Whenever any of these scenarios happen, the body mounts an instantaneous defense, sending cells and natural chemicals to assault those nasty flu germs or repair the slight gash in your skin. Scientifically speaking, this response is known as *inflammation*.

"Inflammation has become one of the hottest areas of medical research," wrote Christine Gorman and Alice Park in *Time* magazine. "Hardly a week goes by without the publication of yet another study uncovering a new way that chronic inflammation does harm to the body. It destabilizes cholesterol deposits in the coronary arteries, leading to heart attacks."[1]

Most people think inflammation is something that happens to your back after digging up weeds all Saturday morning. Actually inflammation occurs internally as well. When viruses invade the respiratory system by your breathing in toxins from the air, or the digestive system by your wolfing down a bad hot dog from the street vendor, the body launches a counterattack that lays waste to evil intruders or repairs any infected bodily organs.

When inflammation occurs, the liver produces a high-sensitivity C-reactive protein. This natural chemical is released into the bloodstream to help the body fight flu germs, for example, or repair itself after you pull a splinter out of your index finger. What medical researchers are learning, however, is that high C-reactive protein levels can be a warning sign of an impending heart attack. This is noteworthy because only 50 percent of the people who have heart attacks in the U.S. have normal or moderately elevated cholesterol levels.

High levels of C-reactive protein may also explain why people with low cholesterol develop heart disease in the first place. My third key, "Practice Advanced Hygiene," can protect your body from becoming chronically inflamed, which will lower your C-reactive protein levels as well as lower your risk of developing heart disease.

What do I mean by the phrase "advanced hygiene"?

I'm glad you asked because I'm a great believer in protecting myself from harmful germs, and I've been practicing an advanced hygiene protocol for more than a decade. I've witnessed the results in my life: no lingering head colds, no nagging sinus infections, no acute respiratory illnesses to speak of for many years, and a total cholesterol number right where it should be—160 mg/dl.

I follow a program first developed by an Australian scientist, Kenneth Seaton, Ph.D., who discovered that ear, nose, throat, and skin problems could be linked to the fact that humans touch their noses, eyes, and mouths with germ-carrying fingernails throughout the day.

In scientific terms, this is known as auto- or self-inoculation. If you thought that most germs were spread by airborne exposure—someone sneezing at your table—you would be wrong. "Germs don't fly, they hitchhike," Dr. Seaton declared, and I believe he's right.

Dr. Seaton estimates that once you pick up hitchhiking germs, they hibernate and hide around the fingernails, no matter how short you keep them trimmed. How do you get germs on your hands? By shaking hands with others or touching things they touched: handrails, doorknobs, shopping carts, paper money, coins, and food. I know this stuff isn't pleasant dinner-time conversation, but practicing advanced hygiene has become an everyday habit for me.

Since I'm aware that 90 percent of germs take up residence around my fingernails, I use a creamy semisoft soap rich in essential oils. Each morning and evening, I dip both of my hands into the tub of semisoft soap and dig my fingernails into the cream. Then I work the special cream around the tips of fingers, cuticles, and fingernails for fifteen to thirty seconds. When I'm finished, I rinse my hands under running water. After my hands are clean, I take another dab of semisoft soap and wash my face.

My next step involves a procedure that I call a "facial dip." I fill my washbasin or a clean large bowl with warm but not hot water. When enough water is in the basin, I add one to two tablespoons of regular table salt and two eyedroppers of a mineral-based facial solution to the cloudy water. I mix everything with my hands and then I bend over and dip my face into the cleansing matter, opening my eyes several times to allow the membranes to be cleansed. After coming up for air, I dunk my head a second time and blow bubbles through my nose. "Sink snorkeling," I call it.

My final two steps of advanced hygiene involve the application of very diluted drops of hydrogen peroxide and minerals into my ears for thirty to sixty seconds to cleanse the ear canal, followed by brushing my teeth with an essential oil–based tooth solution to cleanse my teeth, gums, and mouth of unhealthy germs. (For a listing of my favorite advanced hygiene products, visit www.BiblicalHealthInstitute.com and click on the Resource Guide.)

Brushing your teeth well and regularly practicing advanced hygiene require discipline; you have to remind yourself to do both until they become ingrained habits. I find it easier to follow these steps in the morning when I'm freshly awake than later in the evening when I'm tired and bleary eyed—although I do my best to practice advanced hygiene mornings and evenings and hardly ever miss.

Finally there's another reason why you should practice advanced hygiene, and it has to do with human skin, which is rich in cholesterol. Dr. Seaton, in his book *Life, Health, and Longevity,* noted that the lipids in skin contain a high percentage of cholesterol to prevent infection, but many soaps can wash away these important skin lipids. This explains the importance of using a creamy semisoft soap rich in essential oils that does not contain antibiotic substances.

Regarding the buildup of cholesterol in the arteries, Dr. Seaton said that you should know about a protein floating around in your bloodstream, and it happens to be the most abundant one. It's called albumin, and this protein transports hormones, nutrients, and wastes in your bloodstream. Like dump trucks on their way to the landfill, albumin hauls wastes and toxic cells to the liver for degradation and elimination from the body.

Medical researchers, Dr. Seaton says, have also discovered another interesting bit of news: high albumin levels may be critical to the prevention of diseases like cardiovascular disease and keeping cholesterol levels in check. Those with a history of high cholesterol may have low albumin levels, and "recent studies suggest that this damage can be enhanced in the presence of low serum albumin," said Dr. Seaton. How this relates to heart disease is still being researched, but doctors believe that those with low albumin levels *before* a heart attack strikes could be at greater risk.[2]

Dr. Seaton is certain that albumin levels are linked to *hygiene,* not diet, meaning that albumin levels can be optimized by practicing advanced hygiene, which underscores the importance of this key as part of the Great Physician's prescription for high cholesterol.

A Primer on Washing Your Hands

1. Wet your hands with warm water. It doesn't have to be anywhere near scalding hot.

2. Apply plenty of soap into the palms of both hands. The best soap to use is a semisoft soap that you can dig your fingernails into.

3. Rub your hands vigorously together and scrub all the surfaces. Pay attention to the skin between the fingers and work the soap into the fingernails.

4. Rub and scrub for fifteen to thirty seconds, or about the time it takes to slowly sing "Happy Birthday."

5. Rinse well and dry your hands on a paper towel or clean cloth towel. If you're in a public restroom, it's a good idea to turn off the running water with the towel in your hand. An even *better* idea is to use that same towel to open the door since that door handle is the first place that non-washers touch after they've gone to the bathroom.

6. Keep waterless sanitizers in your purse or wallet in case soap and water are not available in the public restroom. These towelettes, although not ideal, are better than nothing.

R℞ THE GREAT PHYSICIAN'S RX FOR HIGH CHOLESTEROL: PRACTICE ADVANCED HYGIENE

- *Dig your fingers into a semisoft soap with essential oils and wash your hands regularly, paying special attention to removing germs from underneath your fingernails.*

- *Cleanse your nasal passageways and the mucous membranes of the eyes daily by performing a facial dip.*

- *Cleanse the ear canals at least twice per week.*

- *Use an essential oil-based tooth solution daily to remove germs from the teeth, gums, and mouth.*

Take Action

To learn how to incorporate the principles of practicing advanced hygiene into your daily lifestyle, please turn to page 76 for the Great Physician's Rx for High Cholesterol Battle Plan.

KEY #4

*Condition Your Body
with Exercise and Body Therapies*

I don't normally jump to conclusions, but if you last exercised when Milli Vanilli was filling arenas with chart-topping hits, or your main form of burning calories is toggling the TV remote with your right thumb, I could get pretty good odds in Las Vegas that your total cholesterol number is too high.

You're going to have to pull yourself off the couch and get your body moving because consistent physical exercise is an essential part of the Great Physician's prescription for high cholesterol and reduces levels of potentially harmful cholesterol in the blood, according to researchers at the Duke University Medical Center.[1] Exercising at moderate or high intensities triggers biochemical changes in your body to lower bad LDL cholesterol and boost good HDL levels. For every point gained in your HDL count, the risk of heart disease declines by 3 percent for women and 2 percent for men.[2]

But even light exercise like walking can send cholesterol numbers in the right direction. Researchers followed sixty women who walked three miles a day, five days a week, for six months. Some walked at a fast clip (covering a mile in twelve brisk minutes) while others sauntered along (covering a mile in more leisurely twenty minutes), but each woman walker boosted good HDL levels by around 6 percent.[3] Walking is especially good for those

51

who've been lax in working out over the years. This low-impact route to fitness places a gentle strain on the hips and the rest of the body, and when done briskly, it makes the heart work harder and expend more energy.

I have a background in physical fitness, having been a certified fitness trainer. If you were my client, who had been told by your doctor that you have high cholesterol, I would urge you to start walking as well as get you started on an exercise program called *functional fitness.* This form of mild exercise raises your heartbeat, strengthens the body's core muscles, and exercises the cardiovascular system through the performance of real-life activities in real-life positions.

Functional fitness can be done with no equipment or by employing dumbbells, mini trampolines, and stability balls. You can find functional fitness classes and equipment at gyms around the country, including LA Fitness, Bally Total Fitness, and local YMCAs. You'll be asked to perform squats with feet apart, feet together, and one back with the other forward. What you *won't* be asked to perform are high-impact exercises like those found in pulsating aerobics classes. (For more information on functional fitness, visit www.GreatPhysiciansRx.com.)

I would also incorporate these forms of exercise and body therapies:

1. Rebounders, which look like mini trampolines, are great for low-impact exercise and burn more calories than jogging. Rebounding lowers cholesterol naturally by increasing oxygenation and dilating the blood vessels for smoother and easier blood

flow, according to my friend Morton Walker, DPM, author of *Jumping for Health* and one of the first persons to interview me about my recovery from a chronic, "incurable" digestive disease that affected my entire body when I was a nineteen-year-old college student.

2. Deep-breathing exercises enrich the cardiovascular system. Most of the time, we don't completely fill the diaphragm with air because we're not aware that our lungs hang all the way toward the bottom of the rib cage. I recommend sitting in a chair and concentrating on filling the lungs completely. Count to five as you breathe in, then hold your breath for up to four seconds before exhaling through your mouth for several more seconds.

3. Go to bed earlier. Sleep is a body therapy in short supply these days. A nationwide sleep deficit means that we're packing in as much as we can from the moment we wake up until we crawl into bed sixteen, seventeen, or eighteen exhausting hours later. American adults are down to a little less than seven hours of sleep each night, a good two hours less than our great-great-grandparents slept a hundred years ago. This can't be good for the heart.

How many hours of sleep are you getting nightly? The magic number is eight hours, say the sleep experts. That's because when people are allowed to sleep as much as they would like in a controlled setting—for example, in a sleep laboratory—they naturally sleep eight hours in a twenty-four-hour time period.

This is a good time to talk about sleep apnea and how it

relates to cholesterol. First of all, sleep apnea is a serious, potentially life-threatening condition characterized by brief interruptions in breathing during sleep. Those with sleep apnea are often unaware that they wheeze and snore throughout the night, only to have their breathing suddenly stop for a long moment.

German researchers led by Jan Börgel, M.D., discovered that the more severe the apnea, the lower the level of good HDL cholesterol in the blood, which only underscores the importance of treating this syndrome.[4] Standard apnea treatment calls for using a special pressure-generating machine that blows air into the airways to stop them from collapsing. Those who used this machine, according to German researchers, experienced a falling in their total cholesterol, bad LDL cholesterol, and triglyceride levels.

So, if your snoring knocks family photos off the wall, or your spouse comments about momentary pauses in your breathing, that's a good sign that you need to seek medical attention for sleep apnea.

4. Rest on the seventh day. In addition to proper sleep, the body needs a time of rest every seven days to recharge its batteries. This is accomplished by taking a break from the rat race on Saturday or Sunday. God created the earth and the heavens in six days and rested on the seventh, giving us an example and a reminder that we need to take a break from our labors. Otherwise, we're prime candidates for burnout.

5. Let the sun shine in. Remember how I mentioned in Key #2 that cod-liver oil contains high levels of vitamin D, which plays a

role in immunity, reduces inflammation, and ensures healthy blood cell formation? When your face, arms, and legs are exposed to sunlight, your skin synthesizes vitamin D from the ultraviolet rays of the sun. That's why I recommend intentionally exposing yourself to at least fifteen minutes of sunlight a day—preferably before 10:00 a.m. or after 2:00 p.m.—to increase vitamin D levels in the body.

6. Treat yourself to hydrotherapy. Hydrotherapy comes in the form of baths, showers, washing, and wraps—using hot *and* cold water. For instance, I wake up with a hot shower in the mornings, but then I turn off the hot water and stand under the brisk cold water for about a minute, which totally invigorates me. Cold water stimulates the body and boosts oxygen use in the cells, while hot water dilates blood vessels, which improves blood circulation and transports more oxygen to the brain.

A great way to detoxify the body of harmful environmental chemicals, fat-soluble toxins, and heavy metals is the regular use of a far infrared sauna. Far infrared saunas provide a comfortable and simple way to boost cardiovascular circulation, and regular users have reported an improvement in skin tone and a lessening of aches and pains. I have owned and used a far infrared sauna for more than eight years and highly recommend it. (For more information on far infrared sauna technology, visit www.BiblicalHealthInstitute.com.)

7. Pamper yourself with aromatherapy and music therapy. In aromatherapy, essential oils from plants, flowers, and spices are

introduced to your skin and pores either by rubbing them in or by inhaling their aromas. The use of these essential oils will not miraculously repair blocked coronary arteries, but they will give you an emotional lift. Try rubbing a few drops of myrtle, coriander, hyssop, galbanum, or frankincense onto the palms, then cup your hands over your mouth and nose and inhale. A deep breath will invigorate the body, mind, and spirit.

So will listening to soft and soothing music that promotes relaxation and healing. I know what I like when it comes to music therapy: contemporary praise and worship music. No matter what works for you, you'll find that listening to uplifting "mood" music can heal the body, soul, and spirit.

R͟x THE GREAT PHYSICIAN'S RX FOR HIGH CHOLESTEROL: CONDITION YOUR BODY WITH EXERCISE AND BODY THERAPIES

- *Make a commitment and an appointment to exercise three times a week or more for a total of at least three hours of physical activity per week.*

- *Incorporate five to fifteen minutes of functional fitness into your daily schedule.*

- *Take a brisk walk and see how much better you feel at the end of the day.*

- Make a conscious effort to practice deep-breathing exercises once a day. Inflate your lungs to full and hold for several seconds before slowly exhaling.

- Each Saturday or Sunday, take a day of rest. Dedicate the day to the Lord and do something fun and relaxing that you haven't done in a while. Make your rest day work-free, errand-free, and shop-free. Trust God that He'll do more with His six days than you can do with seven.

- Go to sleep earlier, paying close attention to how much sleep you get before midnight. Do your best to get eight hours of sleep nightly. Remember that sleep is the most important nonnutrient you can incorporate into your health regimen.

- End your shower by changing the water temperature to cool (or cold) and standing underneath the spray for one minute.

- Sit outside in a chair and face the sun every day. Soak up the rays for ten or fifteen minutes.

- Incorporate essential oils into your daily life.

- Play worship music in your home, in your car, or on your iPod. Focus on God's plan for your life.

Take Action

To learn how to incorporate the principles of conditioning your body with exercise and body therapies into your daily lifestyle, please turn to page 76 for the Great Physician's Rx for High Cholesterol Battle Plan.

KEY #5

Reduce Toxins in Your Environment

One of the unfortunate aspects regarding high cholesterol is that there are no symptoms for this condition, which is why high cholesterol is sometimes referred to as "the silent killer," a title also given to hypertension, or high blood pressure.

You were probably not aware that you had elevated cholesterol until you took a blood test during a routine office visit with your family physician. Well, if you had your blood and urine tested for various chemicals and toxins inside your body, I have another surprise waiting for you: lab technicians would likely uncover dozens of toxins in your bloodstream, including PCBs (polychlorinated biphenyls), dioxins, furans, trace metals, phthalates, VOCs (volatile organic compounds), and chlorine. Scientists refer to this chemical residue as a person's *body burden.*

Although our bodies are designed to eliminate toxins, our immune systems have become overloaded because of the chemicals and toxins present in the foods we eat, the air we breathe, and the water we drink. Some toxins are water soluble, meaning they are rapidly passed out of the body and present no harm. Unfortunately many more toxins are fat soluble, meaning that it can take months or years before they are completely eliminated from your system. Some of the more well known fat-soluble toxins are dioxins, phthalates, and chlorine, and when they are not eliminated from the body, they become stored in your fatty tissues and can lead to clogged arteries.

The best way to flush fat-soluble toxins out of your bloodstream is to increase your intake of drinking water, which helps eliminate toxins through the kidneys. You must increase the fiber in your diet to eliminate toxins through the bowel, exercise and sweat to eliminate toxins through the lymphatic system, and practice deep breathing to eliminate toxins through the lungs.

Another way to reduce the number of toxins—as well as push your cholesterol numbers in the right direction—is to consume organic or grass-fed meat and dairy products. Remember: most commercially produced beef, chicken, and pork act as chemical magnets for toxins in the environment, so they will not be as healthy as eating grass-fed beef. In addition, consuming organic produce purchased at health food stores, roadside stands, and farmers' markets (only if produce is grown locally and unsprayed) will expose you to less pesticide residues, as compared to conventionally grown fruits and vegetables.

Typical canned tuna is another food to eat minimally, although many popular diets include tuna and salad as a lunchtime or dinner staple. Metallic particles of mercury, lead, and aluminum continue to be found in the fatty tissues of tuna, swordfish, and king mackerel. However, there is now a canned tuna available that is not only low in mercury but extremely high in heart-healthy omega-3 fatty acids. This tuna can be safely consumed many times per week and contains nearly twice the amount of omega-3 fats (such as EPA and DHA) as fatty fish such as salmon and sardines. (For information on low mercury, high omega-3 tuna, visit www.BiblicalHealthInstitute.com and click on the Resource Guide.)

WHAT TO DRINK

I've already touted the healthy benefits of drinking water in Key #1, but when it comes to reducing toxins in your environment, water is especially important because of its ability to flush out toxins and other metabolic wastes from the body. The importance of drinking enough water cannot be overstated: water is a life force involved in nearly every bodily process, from digestion to blood circulation. Your heart pumps blood much more efficiently when you're well hydrated because the blood is thinner. If you have too much cholesterol, your arteries could be narrowed, which slows down or even blocks blood flow. Result: the heart receives less oxygen.

Remember Dr. Batmanghelidj's provocative statement: excess cholesterol is the result of dehydration. "It is the dehydration that causes many different diseases and not the level of cholesterol in the circulating blood," he said.[1] The answer to hydration is plain old water—a liquid created by God to be totally compatible with your body. You should be drinking the proverbial eight glasses of water daily as a minimum.

I know what you're thinking: *Jordan, if I drink that much water, I can never be farther than fifteen steps from a bathroom.* Yes, you will probably treble your trips to the toilet, but trust me on this: if you're serious about your cholesterol, you must be serious about drinking enough water. There's no other physiological way for you to rid yourself of chemicals and toxins stored inside your body.

I don't recommend drinking water straight from the tap, however. Nearly all municipal water is routinely treated with chlorine or chloramine, potent bacteria-killing chemicals. I've installed a whole-house filtration system that removes the chlorine and other impurities from the water *before* it enters our household pipes. My wife, Nicki, and I can confidently turn on the tap and enjoy the health benefits of chlorine-free water for drinking, cooking, and bathing. Since our water doesn't have a chemical aftertaste, we're more apt to drink it.

When I'm at the office or out and about, I sip on bottled water all day long. My feelings are that given a choice, you're better off purchasing bottled water from a natural spring source, although filtered tap water (Dasani and Aquafina, for example) would be okay, too. My favorite bottled water brands are Mountain Valley Spring Water and Trinity Springs Water, which come from natural springs and contain a high mineral content, making them highly alkaline. (For more information on my favorite bottled waters, see the Resource Guide, at www.BiblicalHealthInstitute.com.)

Don't think the answer to good hydration is found in diet soft drinks or beverages such as coffee, tea, and fruit juices, even though the latter can be healthy for you. Diet drinks contain artificial sweeteners like aspartame, acesulfame K, or sucralose. Even though the Food and Drug Administration has approved the use of artificial sweeteners in drinks (and foods), in my opinion these chemical food additives may prove to be detrimental to your health in the long term.

Toxins Elsewhere in Your Environment

Other toxins not directly related to high cholesterol are signifi-
cant enough to mention:

- *Household cleaners.* Many of today's commercial household
  cleaners contain potentially harmful chemicals and solvents that expose people to VOCs—volatile organic compounds—which can cause eye, nose, and throat irritation.

  Nicki and I have found that natural ingredients like
  vinegar, lemon juice, and baking soda are excellent substances that make our home spick-and-span. Natural
  cleaning products that aren't harsh, abrasive, or potentially dangerous to your family are available in grocery
  and natural food stores.

- *Skin care and body care products.* Toxic chemicals such as
  chemical solvents and phthalates are found in lipstick, lip
  gloss, lip conditioner, hair coloring, hair spray, shampoo,
  and soap. Ladies, when you rub a tube of lipstick across
  your lips, your skin readily absorbs these toxins, and
  that's unhealthy. As with the case regarding household
  cleaners, you can find natural cosmetics in progressive
  natural food markets, although they are becoming more
  widely available in drugstores and beauty supply stores.

- *Toothpaste.* A tube of toothpaste contains a warning that
  in case of accidental swallowing, you should contact the
  local Poison Control Center. What's that all about? Most

commercially available toothpastes contain artificial sweeteners, potassium nitrate, sodium fluoride, and a whole bunch of long, unpronounceable words. Again, search out a healthy, natural version.

R_X THE GREAT PHYSICIAN'S RX FOR HIGH CHOLESTEROL: REDUCE TOXINS IN YOUR ENVIRONMENT

- *Eat organic meat from grass-fed sources to lower your exposure to environmental toxins.*

- *When eating canned fish, look for low mercury, high omega-3 sources of tuna.*

- *Drink the recommended eight glasses of water daily— or one quart for every fifty pounds of body weight.*

- *Don't use tobacco products.*

- *Improve indoor air quality by opening windows and buying an air filtration system.*

- *Use natural cleaning products for your home.*

- *Use natural products for skin care, body care, hair care, cosmetics, and toothpaste.*

Take Action

To learn how to incorporate the principles of reducing toxins in your environment into your daily lifestyle, please turn to page 76 for the Great Physician's Rx for High Cholesterol Battle Plan.

KEY #6

Avoid Deadly Emotions

Gidget Stous fidgeted with her hands as she waited for her doctor to give her the results of her cholesterol test, as well as a battery of other health assessments.

"The results are not good," her family physician intoned. "I see evidence of hypertension, and you're likely a borderline diabetic. But of graver concern are your cholesterol levels. They are quite elevated for a twenty-seven-year-old woman. Your total serum cholesterol is 278 and your LDL is 195. Your cholesterol/HDL ratio is 5.1, which is also high."

Gidget wasn't sure exactly what those numbers meant, so she asked for an explanation. "How bad are they?" she asked.

"Gidget, let me put it this way: you have the cholesterol level of a sixty-five-year-old woman," her doctor replied. "If you don't do something soon, you won't see your children grow up."

Upon hearing that dramatic statement, Gidget Stous felt her world turn upside down. The stress of divorcing a wandering husband, owning her own insurance agency, and raising two preteen children came crashing down onto her shoulders. Years of snacking on cookies left at the office, eating every scrap of delicious food on her plate when she lunched with the "girls," and not denying herself at the holiday buffet tables had come home to roost. At 230 pounds, she had let herself go too far. She knew that when she had gathered up the courage to look at herself in a full-length mirror.

High cholesterol wasn't her only health challenge. Her chart revealed other afflictions: acid reflux, allergies, hypertension, and a "female problem"—endometriosis. "I had really low energy, was miserable, and was terribly stressed about everything happening in my life," she told me after I met her while speaking at a church in Kansas City, Missouri.

Things began to turn around when she began dating a fellow named Mike. Her boyfriend gave her one of my earlier books to read—*The Maker's Diet*—but she put the book aside for several months until she finally began reading it one evening.

When she came to the section on how I don't eat pork because God didn't design our bodies to eat scavenger animals, Gidget's immediate reaction was, "No way." She had an emotional attachment to bacon on her breakfast plate and pork chops with mashed potatoes and gravy for dinner. That was how she was raised.

Then she was hit between the eyes with the news that she had the cholesterol level of a sixty-five-year-old woman. Over the next few months, Gidget made lifestyle changes that come straight out of the Great Physician's prescription for high cholesterol. She exchanged the half-dozen Cokes she drank at her desk for bottled water. She stopped eating processed foods and unclean meats. She married Mike, and after setting up house together, she and her new husband and the children volunteered to do chores at a nearby farm in exchange for raw milk, free-range eggs, real butter, and grass-fed beef and chicken. Following the advanced hygiene program of morning and evening facial dips took care of her allergies.

In less than six months, she lost eighty-five pounds. "Many of my longtime customers at the office didn't recognize me when

I got down to 140 pounds. After the extra weight went away, so did my stress and my high cholesterol," Gidget told me.

There was another deadly emotion, however, that Gidget had to deal with—unforgiveness. Her first husband had an affair, which devastated her self-esteem and destroyed her marriage. When she added weight following the births of her children, acquaintances made subtle digs: "Are you really going to eat that?" or "Have you thought about trying this diet?"

"These women were the most insensitive to me," Gidget said. "They'd make these little remarks while they were eating the same junk at lunch."

Gidget did something that I recommend for people dealing with unforgiveness in their hearts. She wrote down the name of her ex-husband as well as the names of those who had made cutting remarks about her weight and appearance over the years. Next to each name she listed each grievance they had brought against her. Then she asked God to help her forgive them, followed by crumpling up the paper and tossing it into the trash. "I had issues with people who were mean to me, including family members," Gidget said. "One way or another, I had to forgive them because otherwise I'd become too stressed over the whole thing."

What about you? Are you harboring resentment in your heart, nursing a grudge into overtime, or plotting revenge against those who hurt you? If you're still bottling up emotions such as anger, bitterness, and resentment, these deadly emotions will produce toxins similar to bingeing on a dozen glazed doughnuts. The efficiency of your immune system decreases noticeably for six hours, and staying angry and bitter about those who have teased you in the past can alter the chemistry of your body—and even prompt you to fall off the healthy food wagon again. An old proverb states it well: "What you are eating is not nearly as important as what's eating you."

This is not the time to revert to old habits: consuming a deep-dish large pizza in one sitting, scarfing a package of cookies, or plying yourself with "pleasure" foods filled with fat and sugar. If you're still annoyed by those who teased you about your body shape, made snide comments about your plus-size clothes, or told you that you'll never lose weight, you have to let it go. Sure, they were mean to you, but that's history.

As much as she had been hurt, Gidget put her past in the rearview mirror and moved forward. Following the Great Physician's Rx for a healthy lifestyle helped her deal with the deadly emotions weighing her down. As for you, please remember that no matter how badly you've been hurt in the past, it's still possible to forgive. Jesus said, "If you forgive men their trespasses, your heavenly Father will also forgive you. But if you do not forgive men their trespasses, neither will your Father forgive your trespasses" (Matt. 6:14–15 NKJV).

Give your forgiveness to those who tormented you, hurt you, and made you angry, and then "let go and let God."

R̵x THE GREAT PHYSICIAN'S RX FOR HIGH CHOLESTEROL: AVOID DEADLY EMOTIONS

- *Don't eat when you're sad, scared, or angry.*

- *Recognize the interaction between deadly emotions and your physical health.*

- *Trust God when you face circumstances that cause you to worry or become anxious.*

- *Practice forgiveness every day and forgive those who hurt you.*

Take Action

To learn how to incorporate the principles of avoiding deadly emotions into your daily lifestyle, please turn to page 76 for the Great Physician's Rx for High Cholesterol Battle Plan.

KEY #7

Live a Life of Prayer and Purpose

At the age of forty-eight, Carol Wootten lay dying in a hospital bed. As I shared in an earlier chapter, she had originally been admitted for a staph infection in her left knee that prevented her from walking, but once she entered the hospital, her body's vital signs plummeted like Enron stock. Pain became her constant companion, and not even morphine could salve the agony she felt.

Lord, if this is the way it's going to be, take me now, she prayed.

Her doctor pulled her husband, Edward, into a nearby room and delivered a jolt of bad news: with her body temperature soaring at 104 degrees, her oxygen level dropping to 78, and other vital signs acting erratically, there was a good chance that Carol wouldn't make it through the night. If anyone wanted to see Carol before she "passed," now was the time.

The doctor ordered Valium to be added to her IV to make her final hours more "comfortable." Carol fell into a deep dream . . . a dream that took her on a long journey . . . to an idyllic place of great beauty and contentment. She sensed that she was entering her final resting spot—heaven.

Carol's countenance brightened. She had believed that Jesus Christ promised her salvation if she trusted in Him, and everything He said was coming true, including eternal life with Him in heaven. She was ready . . . and also looking forward to seeing others who had gone before her.

But then someone met her at the entrance to heaven. "It's not your time," the angelic host said. "You have unfinished business, and you have to go back."

At the same moment Carol was dreaming about what lay beyond, her twenty-three-year-old son, Jeremy, was praying with his youth pastor, Jesse Franco, at Calvary Temple Worship Center in Modesto. After a season of lifting his mother's life to the Lord, the pastor said to her son, "Jeremy, she will be fine. God has something for her to do."

At nearly the same moment Pastor Franco made that declaration, Carol woke up in her hospital bed and looked around. She was still connected to a zillion machines keeping her alive: it looked like heaven could wait. A nurse came in and took her blood pressure and was amazed that it had returned to normal levels. In fact, all her vital signs had stabilized. At that moment, Carol Wootten knew that the Lord—the Author and Giver of life—had granted her another stay on earth.

You can believe that Carol's attitude has changed since she was hospitalized two years ago. "God has something for me to do," she said. "I'm not sure what it is, but I'm excited to find out."

Carol Wootten is living life with a renewed sense of purpose these days. She feels called to pray for others as an intercessor, and that's where she feels God is leading her. What about you? Are you traveling placidly through life, waiting for something to happen, or does your attitude about life belie a purpose about why God created you?

You should feel a sense of purpose every morning when you wake up. If you're not sure what your purpose is, search your heart. What makes you feel alive? What are you passionate about? The joys of family? The arts? Teaching others? Your purpose is waiting to be discovered. Pinpoint your passions, and you'll uncover your purpose. Keep in mind that God gives us different desires, different dreams, and different talents for a reason because we are all part of one body. Having a purpose will give you something to live for.

Whether a sense of purpose fills your heart or you're struggling with why you're here on this earth, I urge you to pray. Prayer is how we talk to God. Prayer is two-way communication with our Creator, the God of the universe. There is no greater source of power than talking to the One who made us. Prayer is not a formality. Prayer is not about religion. Prayer is about a relationship—the hotline to heaven. We can talk to God anytime, anywhere, for any reason. He is always there to listen, and He always has our best interests at heart because we are His children. You'll find that prayer is the foundation of a healthy life, linking your mind, body, and spirit to God.

In living a healthy, purpose-filled life, prayer is the most powerful tool that we possess. Through prayer, God takes away our guilt, shame, bitterness, and anger and gives us a brand-new start. We can eat organic whole foods, supplement our diet with whole food supplements, practice advanced hygiene, exercise, reduce toxins, and deal with deadly emotions, but if our relationship and communication with God are not where they need to be, then we will never be completely healthy. Talking to our Maker through prayer is the foundation for optimal health and makes us whole. After all, God's love and grace are our greatest foods for body, mind, and spirit.

The seventh key to unlocking your health potential is living a life of prayer and purpose. Prayer will confirm your purpose, and it will give you the perseverance to complete it. Seal all that you do with the power of prayer, and watch your life become more than you ever thought possible.

Scripture calls your body the temple of the Holy Spirit. If you're dealing with high cholesterol levels and poor health, you owe it to God—who, according to Scripture, purchased you with a great price—to follow His health principles. He wants to use you to bring heaven to earth and to bring those on earth with you to heaven.

START A SMALL GROUP

It's difficult to face health challenges alone. If you have friends or family members struggling with high cholesterol and poor health, ask them to join you in following the Great Physician's prescription for health and wellness. To learn about joining an existing group in the area or leading a small group in your church, please visit www.GreatPhysiciansRx.com.

R̥ THE GREAT PHYSICIAN'S RX FOR HIGH CHOLESTEROL: LIVE A LIFE OF PRAYER AND PURPOSE

- *Pray continually.*

- *Confess God's promises upon waking and before you retire each night.*

- *Find God's purpose for your life and live it.*

- *Be an agent of change in your life. Only you can take that first step toward better health.*

Take Action

To learn how to incorporate the principles of living a life of prayer and purpose into your daily lifestyle, please turn to page 76 for the Great Physician's Rx for High Cholesterol Battle Plan.

THE GREAT PHYSICIAN'S RX
FOR HIGH CHOLESTEROL
BATTLE PLAN

DAY 1

Upon Waking

Prayer: thank God because this is the day that the Lord has made. Rejoice and be glad in it. Thank Him for the breath in your lungs and the life in your body. Ask the Lord to heal your body and use your experience to benefit the lives of others. Read Matthew 6:9–13 aloud.

Purpose: ask the Lord to give you an opportunity to add significance to someone's life today. Watch for that opportunity. Ask God to use you this day for His intended purpose.

Advanced hygiene: for hands and nails, jab fingers into semisoft soap four or five times, and lather hands with soap for fifteen seconds, rubbing soap over cuticles and rinsing under water as warm as you can stand. Take another swab of semisoft soap into your hands and wash your face. Next, fill basin or sink with water as warm as you can stand, and add one to three tablespoons of table salt and one to three eyedroppers of iodine-based mineral solution. Dunk face into water and open eyes, blinking repeatedly underwater. Keep eyes open underwater for three seconds. After cleaning your eyes, put your face back in the water, and close your mouth while blowing bubbles out of your nose. Come up from the water, and immerse your face in the water once again, gently taking water into your nostrils and expelling bubbles. Come up from the water, and blow your nose into facial tissue. To cleanse the ears, use hydrogen peroxide and mineral-based ear drops, putting two or three drops into each ear and letting it stand for sixty seconds. Tilt your head to expel the drops.

For the teeth, apply two or three drops of essential oil–based tooth drops to the toothbrush. This can be used to brush your teeth or added to existing toothpaste. After brushing your teeth, brush your tongue for fifteen seconds. (For recommended advanced hygiene products, visit www.BiblicalHealthInstitute.com and click on the Resource Guide.)

Reduce toxins: open your windows for one hour today. Use natural soap and natural skin and body care products (shower gel, body creams, etc.). Use natural facial care products. Use natural toothpaste. Use natural hair care products such as shampoo, conditioner, gel, mousse, and hairspray. (For recommended products, visit www.BiblicalHealth Institute.com and click on the Resource Guide.)

Supplements: take one serving of a fiber/green superfood powder (mixed) or five caplets of a supergreen formula swallowed with twelve to sixteen ounces of water or raw vegetable juice (for recommended products, visit www.BiblicalHealthInstitute.com and click on the Resource Guide).

Body therapy: get twenty minutes of direct sunlight sometime during the day, but be careful between the hours of 10:00 a.m. and 2:00 p.m.

Exercise: perform functional fitness exercises for five to fifteen minutes or spend five to fifteen minutes on a mini trampoline. Finish with five to ten minutes of deep-breathing exercises. (One to three rounds of the exercises can be found at www.BiblicalHealthInstitute.com.)

Emotional health: whenever you face a circumstance, such as your health, that causes you to worry, repeat the following: "Lord, I trust You. I cast my cares upon You, and I believe that You're going to take care of [insert your current situation] and make my health and my body strong." Confess that throughout the day whenever you think about your health condition.

Breakfast

Make a smoothie in a blender with the following ingredients:

1 cup organic plain yogurt or kefir (goat's milk is best)

1 tablespoon organic flaxseed oil

1 to 2 tablespoons organic raw honey

1 cup organic fruit (berries, banana, peaches, pineapple, etc.)

2 tablespoons goat's milk protein powder (for recommended brands, visit www.BiblicalHealthInstitute.com and click on the Resource Guide)

dash of vanilla extract (optional)

Supplements: take two whole food multivitamin caplets and one capsule of a whole food antioxidant/energy formula (for recommended brands, visit www.BiblicalHealthInstitute.com and click on the Resource Guide).

Lunch

Before eating, drink eight ounces of water.

During lunch, drink eight ounces of water or hot or iced green tea with honey.

large green salad with mixed greens, avocado, carrots, cucumbers, celery, tomatoes, red cabbage, red peppers, red onions, and sprouts with three hard-boiled omega-3 eggs

salad dressing: mix extra virgin olive oil, apple cider vinegar or lemon juice, minced fresh garlic, naturally brewed soy sauce, Celtic Sea Salt, herbs, and spices; or, mix one tablespoon of extra virgin olive oil with one tablespoon of a healthy store-bought dressing

one apple with skin

Supplements: take two whole food multivitamin caplets and one capsule of a whole food antioxidant/energy formula.

Dinner

Before eating, drink eight ounces of water.

During dinner, drink hot or iced green tea with honey (for recommended brands, visit www.BiblicalHealthInstitute.com and click on the Resource Guide).

baked, poached, or grilled wild-caught salmon

steamed broccoli

large green salad with mixed greens, avocado, carrots, tomato, red cabbage, red onions, red peppers, and sprouts

salad dressing: mix extra virgin olive oil, apple cider vinegar or lemon juice, minced fresh garlic, naturally brewed soy sauce, Celtic Sea Salt, herbs, and spices; or, mix one tablespoon of extra virgin olive oil with one tablespoon of a healthy store-bought dressing

Supplements: take two whole food multivitamin caplets, one capsule of a whole food antioxidant blend, and one to three teaspoons or three to nine capsules of a high omega-3 cod-liver oil complex (for recommended brands, visit www.BiblicalHealthInstitute.com and click on the Resource Guide).

Snacks

apple slices with raw almond butter

one berry antioxidant whole food nutrition bar with beta-glucans from soluble oat fiber (for recommended brands, visit www.Biblical HealthInstitute.com and click on the Resource Guide)

eight to twelve ounces of water or hot or iced green tea with honey (for recommended brands, visit www.BiblicalHealthInstitute.com and click on the Resource Guide)

Before Bed

Exercise: go for a walk outdoors or participate in a favorite sport or recreational activity.

Supplements: take one serving of a fiber/green superfood powder (mixed) or five caplets of a supergreen formula swallowed with twelve to sixteen ounces of water or raw vegetable juice.

Body therapy: take a warm bath for fifteen minutes with eight drops of biblical essential oils added.

Advanced hygiene: repeat the advanced hygiene instructions from the morning of Day 1.

Emotional health: ask the Lord to bring to your mind someone you need to forgive. On a sheet of paper, write the person's name at the top. Try to remember each specific action that person did that brought you pain. Write the following: "I forgive [insert person's name] for [insert the action he or she did]." After you fill up the paper, tear it up or burn it, and ask God to give you the strength to truly forgive that person.

Purpose: ask yourself these questions: "Did I live a life of purpose today?" "What did I do to add value to someone else's life today?" Commit to living a day of purpose tomorrow.

Prayer: thank God for this day, asking Him to give you a restoring night's rest and a fresh start tomorrow. Thank Him for His steadfast love that never ceases and His mercies that are new every morning. Read Romans 8:35, 37–39 aloud.

Sleep: go to bed by 10:30 p.m.

DAY 2

Upon Waking

Prayer: thank God because this is the day that the Lord has made. Rejoice and be glad in it. Thank Him for the breath in your lungs and the life in your body. Ask the Lord to heal your body and use your experience to benefit the lives of others. Read Psalm 91 aloud.

Purpose: ask the Lord to give you an opportunity to add significance to someone's life today. Watch for that opportunity. Ask God to use you this day for His intended purpose.

Advanced hygiene: follow the advanced hygiene recommendations from the morning of Day 1.

Reduce toxins: follow the recommendations to reduce toxins from the morning of Day 1.

Supplements: take one serving of a fiber/green superfood powder (mixed) or five caplets of a supergreen formula swallowed with twelve to sixteen ounces of water or raw vegetable juice.

Body therapy: take a hot and cold shower. After a normal shower, alternate sixty seconds of water as hot as you can stand it, followed by sixty seconds of water as cold as you can stand it. Repeat cycle four times for a total of eight minutes, finishing with cold.

Exercise: perform functional fitness exercises for five to fifteen minutes or spend five to fifteen minutes on a mini trampoline. Finish with five to ten minutes of deep-breathing exercises. (One to three rounds of the exercises can be found at www.BiblicalHealthInstitute.com.)

Emotional health: follow the emotional health recommendations from the morning of Day 1.

Breakfast

two or three eggs any style, cooked in one tablespoon of extra virgin coconut oil (for recommended brands, visit www.Biblical HealthInstitute.com and click on the Resource Guide)

stir-fried onions, garlic, mushrooms, and peppers

one slice of sprouted or yeast-free whole grain bread with almond butter and honey

Supplements: take two whole food multivitamin caplets and one capsule of a whole food antioxidant/energy formula.

Lunch

Before eating, drink eight ounces of water.

During lunch, drink eight ounces of water or hot or iced green tea with honey.

large green salad with mixed greens, avocado, carrots, tomato, red cabbage, red onions, red peppers, and sprouts with two ounces of low mercury, high omega-3 tuna (for recommended brands, visit www.BiblicalHealthInstitute.com and click on the Resource Guide)

salad dressing: mix extra virgin olive oil, apple cider vinegar or lemon juice, minced fresh garlic, naturally brewed soy sauce, Celtic Sea Salt, herbs, and spices; or, mix one tablespoon of extra virgin olive oil with one tablespoon of a healthy store-bought dressing

organic grapes

Supplements: take two whole food multivitamin caplets and one capsule of a whole food antioxidant/energy formula.

Dinner

Before eating, drink eight ounces of water.

During dinner, drink hot or iced green tea with honey.

roasted organic chicken

cooked vegetables (carrots, onions, garlic, peas, etc.)

large green salad with mixed greens, avocado, carrots, tomato, red cabbage, red onions, red peppers, and sprouts

salad dressing: mix extra virgin olive oil, apple cider vinegar or lemon juice, minced fresh garlic, naturally brewed soy sauce, Celtic Sea Salt, herbs, and spices; or, mix one tablespoon of extra virgin olive oil with one tablespoon of a healthy store-bought dressing.

Supplements: take two whole food multivitamin caplets, one capsule of a whole food antioxidant/energy blend, and one to three teaspoons or three to nine capsules of a high omega-3 cod-liver oil complex.

Snacks

one serving of a whole food meal supplement with beta-glucans from soluble oat fiber mixed in twelve to sixteen ounces of water (for recommended brands, visit www.BiblicalHealthInstitute.com and click on the Resource Guide).

one whole food nutrition bar with beta-glucans from soluble oat fiber

eight to twelve ounces of water or hot or iced green tea with honey

Before Bed

Exercise: go for a walk outdoors or participate in a favorite sport or recreational activity.

Supplements: take one serving of a fiber/green superfood powder (mixed) or five caplets of a supergreen formula swallowed with twelve to sixteen ounces of water or raw vegetable juice.

Advanced hygiene: repeat the advanced hygiene instructions from the morning of Day 1.

Emotional health: repeat the emotional health recommendations from Day 1.

Purpose: ask yourself these questions: "Did I live a life of purpose today?" "What did I do to add value to someone else's life today?" Commit to living a day of purpose tomorrow.

Prayer: thank God for this day, asking Him to give you a restoring night's rest and a fresh start tomorrow. Thank Him for His steadfast love that never ceases and His mercies new every morning. Read 1 Corinthians 13:4–8 aloud.

Body therapy: spend ten minutes listening to soothing music before you retire.

Sleep: go to bed by 10:30 p.m.

Day 3

Upon Waking

Prayer: thank God because this is the day that the Lord has made. Rejoice and be glad in it. Thank Him for the breath in your lungs and the life in your body. Ask the Lord to heal your body and use your experience to benefit the lives of others. Read Ephesians 6:13–18 aloud.

Purpose: ask the Lord to give you an opportunity to add significance to someone's life today. Watch for that opportunity. Ask God to use you this day for His intended purpose.

Advanced hygiene: follow the advanced hygiene recommendations from the morning of Day 1.

Reduce toxins: follow the recommendations to reduce toxins from the morning of Day 1.

Supplements: take one serving of a fiber/green superfood powder (mixed) or five caplets of a supergreen formula swallowed with twelve to sixteen ounces of water or raw vegetable juice.

Body therapy: get twenty minutes of direct sunlight sometime during the day, but be careful between the hours of 10:00 a.m. and 2:00 p.m.

Exercise: perform functional fitness exercises for five to fifteen minutes or spend five to fifteen minutes on a mini trampoline. Finish with five to ten minutes of deep-breathing exercises. (One to three rounds of the exercises can be found at www.BiblicalHealthInstitute.com.)

Emotional health: follow the emotional health recommendations from Day 1.

Breakfast

four to eight ounces of organic whole milk yogurt or cottage cheese with fruit (pineapple, peaches, or berries), honey, and a dash of vanilla extract

handful of raw almonds

one cup of hot or iced green tea with honey

Supplements: take two whole food multivitamin caplets and one capsule of a whole food antioxidant/energy formula.

Lunch

Before eating, drink eight ounces of water.

During lunch, drink eight ounces of water or hot or iced green tea with honey.

large green salad with mixed greens, avocado, carrots, tomato, red cabbage, red onions, red peppers, and sprouts with three hard-boiled omega-3 eggs

salad dressing: mix extra virgin olive oil, apple cider vinegar or lemon juice, minced fresh garlic, naturally brewed soy sauce, Celtic Sea Salt, herbs, and spices; or, mix one tablespoon of extra virgin olive oil with one tablespoon of a healthy store-bought dressing

one piece of fruit in season

Supplements: take two whole food multivitamin caplets and one capsule of a whole food antioxidant/energy formula.

Dinner

Before eating, drink eight ounces of water.

During dinner, drink hot or iced green tea with honey.

red meat steak (beef, buffalo, or venison)

steamed broccoli

baked sweet potato with butter

large green salad with mixed greens, avocado, carrots, tomato, red cabbage, red onions, red peppers, and sprouts

salad dressing: mix extra virgin olive oil, apple cider vinegar or lemon juice, minced fresh garlic, naturally brewed soy sauce, Celtic Sea Salt, herbs, and spices; or, mix one tablespoon of extra virgin olive oil with one tablespoon of a healthy store-bought dressing

Supplements: take two whole food multivitamin caplets and one capsule of a whole food antioxidant/energy blend and one to three teaspoons or three to nine capsules of a high omega-3 cod-liver oil complex.

Snacks

healthy chocolate (cacao) snack (for recommended brands, visit www.BiblicalHealthInstitute.com and click on the Resource Guide)

one whole food nutrition bar with beta-glucans from soluble oat fiber

eight to twelve ounces of water or hot or iced green tea with honey

Before Bed

Exercise: go for a walk outdoors or participate in a favorite sport or recreational activity.

Supplements: take one serving of a fiber/green superfood powder (mixed) or five caplets of a supergreen formula swallowed with twelve to sixteen ounces of water or raw vegetable juice.

Body therapy: take a warm bath for fifteen minutes with eight drops of biblical essential oils added.

Advanced hygiene: follow the advanced hygiene instructions from the morning of Day 1.

Emotional health: follow the forgiveness recommendations from the evening of Day 1.

Purpose: ask yourself these questions: "Did I live a life of purpose today?" "What did I do to add value to someone else's life today?" Commit to living a day of purpose tomorrow.

Prayer: thank God for this day, asking Him to give you a restoring night's rest and a fresh start tomorrow. Thank Him for His steadfast love that never ceases and His mercies that are new every morning. Read Philippians 4:4–8, 11–13, 19 aloud.

Sleep: go to bed by 10:30 p.m.

DAY 4

Upon Waking

Prayer: thank God because this is the day that the Lord has made. Rejoice and be glad in it. Thank Him for the breath in your lungs and the life in your body. Read Matthew 6:9–13 aloud.

Purpose: ask the Lord to give you an opportunity to add significance to someone's life today. Watch for that opportunity. Ask God to use you this day for His intended purpose.

Advanced hygiene: follow the advanced hygiene recommendations from Day 1.

Reduce toxins: follow the recommendations for reducing toxins from Day 1.

Supplements: take one serving of a fiber/green superfood powder (mixed) or five caplets of a supergreen formula swallowed with twelve to sixteen ounces of water or raw vegetable juice.

Exercise: perform functional fitness exercises for five to fifteen minutes or spend five to fifteen minutes on a mini trampoline. Finish with five to ten minutes of deep-breathing exercises. (One to three rounds of the exercises can be found at www.BiblicalHealthInstitute.com.)

Body therapy: take a hot and cold shower. After a normal shower, alternate sixty seconds of water as hot as you can stand it, followed by sixty seconds of water as cold as you can stand it. Repeat cycle four times for a total of eight minutes, finishing with cold.

Emotional health: follow the emotional health recommendations from the morning of Day 1.

Breakfast

three soft-boiled or poached eggs

four ounces of sprouted whole grain cereal with two ounces of whole milk yogurt or goat's milk (for recommended brands, visit www.Biblical HealthInstitute.com and click on the Resource Guide) one cup of hot or iced green tea with honey

Supplements: take two whole food multivitamin caplets and one capsule of a whole food antioxidant/energy formula.

Lunch

Before eating, drink eight ounces of water.

During lunch, drink eight ounces of water or hot tea with honey.

large green salad with mixed greens, avocado, carrots, tomato, red cabbage, red onions, red peppers, and sprouts with three ounces of low mercury, high omega-3 canned tuna

salad dressing: mix extra virgin olive oil, apple cider vinegar or lemon juice, minced fresh garlic, naturally brewed soy sauce, Celtic Sea Salt, herbs, and spices; or, mix one tablespoon of extra virgin olive oil with one tablespoon of a healthy store-bought dressing

one bunch of grapes with seeds

Supplements: take two whole food multivitamin caplets and one capsule of a whole food antioxidant/energy formula.

Dinner

Before eating, drink eight ounces of water.

During dinner, drink hot tea with honey.

grilled chicken breast

steamed veggies

small portion of cooked whole grain (quinoa, amaranth, millet, or brown rice) cooked with one tablespoon of extra virgin coconut oil

large green salad with mixed greens, avocado, carrots, tomato, red cabbage, red onions, red peppers, and sprouts

salad dressing: mix extra virgin olive oil, apple cider vinegar or lemon juice, minced fresh garlic, naturally brewed soy sauce, Celtic Sea

Salt, herbs, and spices; or, mix one tablespoon of extra virgin olive oil with one tablespoon of a healthy store-bought dressing

Supplements: take two whole food multivitamin caplets and two capsules of a whole food antioxidant blend and one to three teaspoons or three to nine capsules of a high omega-3 cod-liver oil complex.

Snacks

apple and carrots with raw almond butter

one whole food nutrition bar with beta-glucans from soluble oat fiber

eight to twelve ounces of water or hot or iced green tea with honey

Before Bed

Drink eight to twelve ounces of water or hot or iced green tea with honey.

Exercise: go for a walk outdoors or participate in a favorite sport or recreational activity.

Supplements: take one serving of a fiber/green superfood powder (mixed) or five caplets of a supergreen formula swallowed with twelve to sixteen ounces of water or raw vegetable juice.

Advanced hygiene: follow the advanced hygiene recommendations from the morning of Day 1.

Emotional health: follow the forgiveness recommendations from the evening of Day 1.

Purpose: ask yourself these questions: "Did I live a life of purpose today?" "What did I do to add value to someone else's life today?" Commit to living a day of purpose tomorrow.

Prayer: thank God for this day, asking Him to give you a restoring night's rest and a fresh start tomorrow. Thank Him for His steadfast love that never ceases and His mercies that are new every morning. Read Romans 8:35, 37–39 aloud.

Body therapy: spend ten minutes listening to soothing music before you retire.

Sleep: go to bed by 10:30 p.m.

DAY 5 (PARTIAL FAST DAY)

Upon Waking

Prayer: thank God because this is the day that the Lord has made. Rejoice and be glad in it. Thank Him for the breath in your lungs and the life in your body. Read Isaiah 58:6–9 aloud.

Purpose: ask the Lord to give you an opportunity to add significance to someone's life today. Watch for that opportunity. Ask God to use you this day for His intended purpose.

Advanced hygiene: follow the advanced hygiene recommendations from Day 1.

Reduce toxins: follow the recommendations for reducing toxins from Day 1.

Supplements: take one serving of a fiber/green superfood powder (mixed) or five caplets of a supergreen formula swallowed with twelve to sixteen ounces of water or raw vegetable juice.

Exercise: perform functional fitness exercises for five to fifteen minutes or spend five to fifteen minutes on a mini trampoline. Finish with five to ten minutes of deep-breathing exercises.

Body therapy: get twenty minutes of direct sunlight sometime during the day, but be careful between the hours of 10:00 a.m. and 2:00 p.m.

Emotional health: follow the emotional health recommendations from the morning of Day 1.

Breakfast

none (partial fast day)

Drink eight to twelve ounces of water.

Lunch

none (partial fast day)

Drink eight to twelve ounces of water.

Dinner

Before eating, drink eight ounces of water.

During dinner, drink hot or iced green tea with honey.

chicken soup (visit www.GreatPhysiciansRx.com for the recipe)

cultured vegetables (for recommended brands, visit www.Biblical HealthInstitute.com and click on the Resource Guide)

large green salad with mixed greens, avocado, carrots, tomato, red cabbage, red onions, red peppers, and sprouts

salad dressing: mix extra virgin olive oil, apple cider vinegar or lemon juice, minced fresh garlic, naturally brewed soy sauce, Celtic Sea Salt, herbs, and spices; or, mix one tablespoon of extra virgin olive oil with one tablespoon of a healthy store-bought dressing

Supplements: take two whole food multivitamin caplets, two capsules of a whole food antioxidant blend, and one to three teaspoons or three to nine capsules of a high omega-3 cod-liver oil complex.

Snacks

none (partial fast day)

Drink eight to twelve ounces of water.

Before Bed

Drink eight to twelve ounces of water or hot or iced green tea with honey.

Exercise: go for a walk outdoors or participate in a favorite sport or recreational activity.

Supplements: take one serving of a fiber/green superfood powder (mixed) or five caplets of a supergreen formula swallowed with twelve to sixteen ounces of water or raw vegetable juice.

Advanced hygiene: follow the advanced hygiene recommendations from the morning of Day 1.

Emotional health: follow the forgiveness recommendations from the evening of Day 1.

Body therapy: take a warm bath for fifteen minutes with eight drops of biblical essential oils added.

Purpose: ask yourself these questions: "Did I live a life of purpose today?" "What did I do to add value to someone else's life today?" Commit to living a day of purpose tomorrow.

Prayer: thank God for this day, asking Him to give you a restoring night's rest and a fresh start tomorrow. Thank Him for His steadfast love that never ceases and His mercies that are new every morning. Read Isaiah 58:6–9 aloud.

Sleep: go to bed by 10:30 p.m.

DAY 6 (REST DAY)

Upon Waking

Prayer: thank God because this is the day that the Lord has made. Rejoice and be glad in it. Thank Him for the breath in your lungs and the life in your body. Read Psalm 23 aloud.

Purpose: ask the Lord to give you an opportunity to add significance to someone's life today. Watch for that opportunity. Ask God to use you this day for His intended purpose.

Advanced hygiene: follow the advanced hygiene recommendations from Day 1.

Reduce toxins: follow the recommendations for reducing toxins from Day 1.

Supplements: take one serving of a fiber/green superfood powder (mixed) or five caplets of a supergreen formula swallowed with twelve to sixteen ounces of water or raw vegetable juice.

Exercise: no formal exercise since it's a rest day.

Body therapies: none since it's a rest day.

Emotional health: follow the emotional health recommendations from the morning of Day 1.

Breakfast

one cup of hot or iced green tea with honey

two or three eggs cooked any style in one tablespoon of extra virgin coconut oil

one grapefruit or orange

handful of almonds

Supplements: take two whole food multivitamin caplets and one capsule of a whole food antioxidant/energy formula.

Lunch

Before eating, drink eight ounces of water.

During lunch, drink eight ounces of water or hot or iced green tea with honey.

large green salad with mixed greens, avocado, carrots, tomato, red cabbage, red onions, red peppers, and sprouts with two ounces of low mercury, high omega-3 canned tuna

salad dressing: mix extra virgin olive oil, apple cider vinegar or lemon juice, minced fresh garlic, naturally brewed soy sauce, Celtic Sea Salt, herbs, and spices; or, mix one tablespoon of extra virgin olive oil with one tablespoon of a healthy store-bought dressing

one organic apple with the skin

Supplements: take two whole food multivitamin caplets and one capsule of a whole food antioxidant/energy formula.

Dinner

Before eating, drink eight ounces of water.

During dinner, drink hot or iced green tea with honey.

roasted organic chicken

cooked vegetables (carrots, onions, peas, etc.)

large green salad with mixed greens, avocado, carrots, tomato, red cabbage, red onions, red peppers, and sprouts

salad dressing: mix extra virgin olive oil, apple cider vinegar or lemon juice, minced fresh garlic, naturally brewed soy sauce, Celtic Sea Salt, herbs, and spices; or, mix one tablespoon of extra virgin olive oil with one tablespoon of a healthy store-bought dressing

Supplements: take two whole food multivitamin caplets, two capsules of a whole food antioxidant/energy blend, and one to three teaspoons or three to nine capsules of a high omega-3 cod-liver oil complex.

Snacks

one serving of high antioxidant berry powder with beta-glucans from soluble oat fiber mixed in eight to twelve ounces of water (for recommended brands, visit www.BiblicalHealthInstitute.com and click on the Resource Guide)

one whole food nutrition bar with beta-glucans from soluble oat fiber

eight to twelve ounces of water or hot or iced green tea with honey

Before Bed

Drink eight to twelve ounces of water or hot tea with honey.

Exercise: go for a walk outdoors or participate in a favorite sport or recreational activity.

Supplements: take one serving of a fiber/green superfood powder (mixed) or five caplets of a supergreen formula swallowed with twelve to sixteen ounces of water or raw vegetable juice.

Advanced hygiene: follow the advanced hygiene recommendations from the morning of Day 1.

Emotional health: follow the forgiveness recommendations from the evening of Day 1.

Purpose: ask yourself these questions: "Did I live a life of purpose today?" "What did I do to add value to someone else's life today?" Commit to living a day of purpose tomorrow.

Prayer: thank God for this day, asking Him to give you a restoring night's rest and a fresh start tomorrow. Thank Him for His steadfast love that never ceases and His mercies that are new every morning. Read Psalm 23 aloud.

Body therapy: spend ten minutes listening to soothing music before you retire.

Sleep: go to bed by 10:30 p.m.

DAY 7

Upon Waking

Prayer: thank God because this is the day that the Lord has made. Rejoice and be glad in it. Thank Him for the breath in your lungs and the life in your body. Read Psalm 91 aloud.

Purpose: ask the Lord to give you an opportunity to add significance to someone's life today. Watch for that opportunity. Ask God to use you this day for His intended purpose.

Advanced hygiene: follow the advanced hygiene recommendations from Day 1.

Reduce toxins: follow the recommendations for reducing toxins from Day 1.

Supplements: take one serving of a fiber/green superfood powder (mixed) or five caplets of a supergreen formula swallowed with twelve to sixteen ounces of water or raw vegetable juice.

Exercise: perform functional fitness exercises for five to fifteen minutes or spend five to fifteen minutes on a mini trampoline. Finish with five to ten minutes of deep-breathing exercises.

Body therapy: get twenty minutes of direct sunlight sometime during the day, but be careful between the hours of 10:00 a.m. and 2:00 p.m.

Emotional health: follow the emotional health recommendations from the morning of Day 1.

Breakfast

Make a smoothie in a blender with the following ingredients:

1 cup plain yogurt or kefir (goat's milk is best)

1 tablespoon organic flaxseed oil

1 to 2 tablespoons organic raw honey

1 cup organic fruit (berries, banana, peaches, pineapple, etc.)

2 tablespoons goat's milk protein powder

dash of vanilla extract (optional)

Supplements: take two whole food multivitamin caplets and one capsule of a whole food antioxidant/energy formula.

Lunch

Before eating, drink eight ounces of water.

During lunch, drink eight ounces of water or hot or iced green tea with honey.

large green salad with mixed greens, avocado, carrots, tomato, red cabbage, red onions, red peppers, and sprouts with three ounces of cold, poached, or canned wild-caught salmon

salad dressing: mix extra virgin olive oil, apple cider vinegar or lemon juice, minced fresh garlic, naturally brewed soy sauce, Celtic Sea Salt, herbs, and spices; or, mix one tablespoon of extra virgin olive oil with one tablespoon of a healthy store-bought dressing

one piece of fruit in season

Supplements: take two whole food multivitamin caplets and one capsule of a whole food antioxidant/energy formula.

Dinner

Before eating, drink eight ounces of water.

During dinner, drink hot tea with honey.

baked or grilled fish of your choice

steamed broccoli

baked sweet potato with butter

large green salad with mixed greens, avocado, carrots, tomato, red cabbage, red onions, red peppers, and sprouts

salad dressing: mix extra virgin olive oil, apple cider vinegar or lemon juice, minced fresh garlic, naturally brewed soy sauce, Celtic Sea Salt, herbs, and spices; or, mix one tablespoon of extra virgin olive oil with one tablespoon of a healthy store-bought dressing

Supplements: take two whole food multivitamin caplets, one capsule of a whole food antioxidant/energy blend, and one to three teaspoons or three to nine capsules of a high omega-3 cod-liver oil complex.

Snacks

apple slices with raw sesame butter (tahini)

one whole food nutrition bar with beta-glucans from soluble oat fiber

eight to twelve ounces of water or hot or iced green tea with honey

Before Bed

Drink eight to twelve ounces of water or hot or iced green tea with honey.

Exercise: go for a walk outdoors or participate in a favorite sport or recreational activity.

Supplements: take one serving of a fiber/green superfood powder (mixed) or five caplets of a supergreen formula swallowed with twelve to sixteen ounces of water or raw vegetable juice.

Advanced hygiene: follow the advanced hygiene recommendations from the morning of Day 1.

Emotional health: follow the forgiveness recommendations from the evening of Day 1.

Body therapy: take a warm bath for fifteen minutes with eight drops of biblical essential oils added.

Purpose: ask yourself these questions: "Did I live a life of purpose today?" "What did I do to add value to someone else's life today?" Commit to living a day of purpose tomorrow.

Prayer: thank God for this day, asking Him to give you a restoring night's rest and a fresh start tomorrow. Thank Him for His steadfast love that never ceases and His mercies that are new every morning. Read 1 Corinthians 13:4–8 aloud.

Sleep: go to bed by 10:30 p.m.

DAY 8 AND BEYOND

If you're feeling better, you can repeat the Great Physician's Rx for High Cholesterol Battle Plan as many times as you'd like. For detailed step-by-step suggestions and meal and lifestyle plans, visit www.GreatPhysiciansRx.com and join the 40 Day Health Experience for continued good health. Or, you may be interested in the Lifetime of Wellness plan if you want to maintain your newfound level of health. These online programs will provide you with customized daily meal and exercise plans and give you the tools to track your progress.

Need Recipes?

For a detailed list of over two hundred healthy and delicious recipes contained in the Great Physician's Rx eating plan, please visit www.BiblicalHealthInstitute.com.

NOTES

Introduction

1. "High blood cholesterol," MayoClinic.com,
   http://www.mayoclinic.com/health/high-blood-cholesterol/DS00178
   (accessed April 5, 2007).

2. "Twenty-Year Trends in Serum Cholesterol, Hypercholesterolemia, and
   Cholesterol Medication Use. The Minnesota Heart Survey," *Circulation* 112
   (2005): 3884–89,
   http://www.americanheart.org/presenter.jhtml?identifier=3036361 (accessed
   April 5, 2007).

3. "Cardiovascular statistics updated for 2005: New data on risk factors in
   America's youth," American Heart Association,
   http://www.americanheart.org/presenter.jhtml?identifier=3027696 (accessed
   April 5, 2007).

4. Sandra Blakeslee, "Surgeon Questions Cholesterol Role," *New York Times*,
   April 9, 1987.

5. "Why Don't You Include Cholesterol Counts with Your Recipes?"
   Lowcarbezine!, http://www.holdthetoast.com/httblog/archives/000158.html
   (accessed April 5, 2007).

6. Michael Murray, ND, Joseph Pizzorno, ND, and Lara Pizzorno, MA, *The
   Encyclopedia of Healing Foods* (New York: Atria Books, 2005), 701.

7. Alex Berenson, "Lipitor or Generic? Billion-Dollar Battle Looms," *New York
   Times*, October 15, 2005.

8. Benjamin M. Scirica, M.D., and Christopher P. Cannon, M.D., "Treatment of
   Elevated Cholesterol," *Circulation* 111 (2005): e360–e363,
   http://circ.ahajournals.org/cgi/content/full/111/21/e360 (accessed April 5, 2007).

9. Philip J. Hilts, "Drug's Problems Raise Questions on Warnings," *New York
   Times*, August 21, 2001.

10. Michael Murray, ND, and Joseph Pizzorno, ND, *Encyclopedia of Natural Medicine* (New York: Three Rivers Press, 1998), 356–57.

Key #1

1. Uffe Ravnskov, M.D., Ph.D., *The Cholesterol Myths* (Washington, D.C.: New Trend Publishing, 2000), 4–5.

2. Ibid., 5.

3. Uffe Ravnskov, M.D., Ph.D., The Cholesterol Myths, http://www.ravnskov.nu/cholesterol.htm.

4. *Encyclopedia of Natural Healing* (Burnaby, B.C., Canada: Alive Publishing Group, 1997), 583.

5. Murray, Pizzorno, and Pizzorno, *The Encyclopedia of Healing Foods*, 704.

6. F. B. Hu, M. J. Stampfer, E. B. Rimm, et al., "A Prospective Study of Egg Consumption and Risk of Cardiovascular Disease in Men and Women," *Journal of the American Medical Association* 281 (1999): 1387–94.

7. James F. Balch, M.D., and Mark Stengler, ND, *Prescription for Natural Cures* (Hoboken, N.J.: John Wiley & Sons, 2004), 149.

8. *FDA Consumer* magazine, July-August 1997, Publication No. 97-2313.

9. "Whole Grains Help Your Heart," *American Journal of Clinical Nutrition* 80 (December 2004): 1492–99, http://www.wholegrainscouncil.org/research.htm (accessed April 5, 2007).

10. "Fiber May Reduce Women's Risk of Heart Disease," July 1, 1999, CNN.com, http://www.cnn.com/HEALTH/heart/9906/01/heart.fiber/ (accessed April 11, 2007).

11. "Omega-3 Fatty Acids," WholeHealthMD.com, http://www.wholehealthmd.com/ME2/dirmod.asp?sid=17E09E7CFFF64044 8FFB0B4FC1B7FEF0&nm=Reference+Library&type=AWHN_Supplement s&mod=Supplements&mid=&id=034025EFA41345DA9594F677FD339F5 5&tier=2 (accessed April 11, 2007).

12. Murray, Pizzorno, and Pizzorno, *The Encyclopedia of Healing Foods*, 704.

13. Gavin AD, Struthers AD, "Allopurinol reduces B-type natriuretic peptide concentrations and haemoglobin but does not alter exercise capacity in chronic heart failure," *Heart* 91, no. 6 (June 2005): 749–53.

14. L. Djousse, D. K. Arnett, H. Coon, M. A. Province, L. L. Moore, and R. C. Ellison, "Fruit and Vegetable Consumption and LDL Cholesterol: The National Heart, Lung, and Blood Institute Family Heart Study," *American Journal of Clinical Nutrition* 79 (2004): 213–17.

15. Avocado Cholesterol Lowering cholesterol with avocado fat," All-About-Lowering-Cholesterol.com, http://www.all-about-lowering-cholesterol.com/avocado-cholesterol-and-avocado-fat.html (accessed April 5, 2007).

16. "Garlic and Cholesterol," Medical College of Wisconsin HealthLink, http://healthlink.mcw.edu/article/970004118.html (accessed April 5, 2007).

17. Murray and Pizzorno, *Encyclopedia of Natural Medicine*, 356–57.

18. Ron Rosedale, M.D., *The Rosedale Diet* (New York: HarperCollins, 2004), 91.

19. F. Batmanghelidj, M.D., *You're Not Sick, You're Thirsty!* (New York: Warner Books, 2003), 206.

20. "Green Tea," University of Maryland Medical Center, http://www.umm.edu/altmed/ConsHerbs/GreenTeach.html (accessed April 5, 2007).

21. J. T. Braaten, P. J. Wood, F. W. Scott, M. S. Wolynetz, M. K. Lowe, P. Bradley-White, and M. W. Collins, "Oat Beta-glucan Reduces Blood Cholesterol Concentration in Hypercholesterolemic Subjects," *European Journal of Clinical Nutrition* 48, no. 7 (July 1994): 465–74.

22. Balch and Stengler, *Prescription for Natural Cures,* 150.

23. Sally Fallon and Mary G. Enig, Ph.D., "Soy: The Dark Side of America's Favorite 'Health' Food," The Weston A. Price Foundation, http://www.westonaprice.org/soy/darkside.html (accessed April 5, 2007).

Key #2

1. "Niacin," Wikipedia http://en.wikipedia.org/wiki/Niacin (accessed April 5, 2007).

2. David Schardt, "Cholesterol-Lowering Supplements," *Nutrition Action Health Letter* (US ed.), November 1997, http://www.cspinet.org/nah/novnah.htm (accessed April 5, 2007).

3. Krispin Sullivan, C.N., "Cod Liver Oil: The Number One Superfood," The Weston A. Price Foundation, http://www.westonaprice.org/basicnutrition/codliveroil.html (accessed April 5, 2007).

4. "Study Shows Grape Seed Extract May Be Effective in Reducing Blood Pressure," Science Daily, http://www.sciencedaily.com/releases/2006/03/060327084242.htm (accessed April 5, 2007).

5. M. Aviram, L. Dornfeld, M. Kaplan, R. Coleman, D. Gaitini, S. Nitecki, A. Hofman, M. Rosenblat, N. Volkova, D. Presser, J. Attias, T. Hayek, and B. Fuhrman, "Pomegranate Juice Flavonoids Inhibit Low-density Lipoprotein Oxidation and Cardiovascular Diseases: Studies in Atherosclerotic Mice and in Humans," *Drugs Under Experimental and Clinical Research* 28, nos. 2–3 (2002): 49–62.

6. Jessica Pasley, "Drink More Tea to Lower Cholesterol: VUMC Study," Vanderbilt Medical Center, http://www.mc.vanderbilt.edu/reporter/ index.html?ID=2745 (accessed April 5, 2007).

Key #3

1. Christine Gorman and Alice Park, "Inflammation Is a Secret Killer: The Surprising Link Between Inflammation and Asthma, Heart Attacks, Cancer, Alzheimer's and Other Diseases," *Time*, February 23, 2004.

2. Kenneth Seaton, *Life, Health, and Longevity* (Huntington, West Virginia: Kenneth E. Seaton, 1994), 48.

Key #4

1. Duke University Medical Center, "Beneficial Effect of Exercise on Cholesterol Levels Persists After Exercise Cessation," press release, May 28, 2003.

2. Paula Rasich, "High Cholesterol? Let Exercise Work Its Magic," Prevention.com, http://www.prevention.com/article/0,5778,s1-1-75-275-2687-1,00.html (accessed April 5, 2007).

3. Ibid.

4. J. Börgel, B. M. Sanner, A. Bittlinsky, et al., "Obstructive Sleep Apnea and Its Therapy Influence High-density Lipoprotein Cholesterol Serum Levels," *European Respiratory Journal* 27 (2006): 121–27.

Key #5

1. F. Batmanghelidj, M.D., *Your Body's Many Cries for Water* (Falls Church, Va.: Global Health Solutions, 1997), 88–89.

ABOUT THE AUTHORS

Jordan Rubin has dedicated his life to transforming the health of God's people one life at a time. He is the founder and chairman of Garden of Life, Inc., a health and wellness company based in West Palm Beach, Florida, that produces organic functional foods, whole food nutritional supplements and personal care products, and he is a much-in-demand speaker on various health topics.

He and his wife, Nicki, are the parents of a toddler-aged son, Joshua. They make their home in Palm Beach Gardens, Florida.

Joseph D. Brasco, M.D., who has extensive knowledge and experience in gastroenterology and internal medicine, attended medical school at Medical College of Wisconsin in Milwaukee, Wisconsin, and is board certified with the American Board of Internal Medicine. Besides writing for various medical journals, he is also the coauthor of *Restoring Your Digestive Health* with Jordan Rubin. Dr. Brasco is currently in private practice in Huntsville, Alabama.

BHI

BIBLICAL HEALTH
INSTITUTE

The Biblical Health Institute (www.BiblicalHealthInstitute.com) is an online learning community housing educational resources and curricula reinforcing and expanding on Jordan Rubin's Biblical Health message.

Biblical Health Institute provides:

1. "101" level **FREE**, introductory courses corresponding to Jordan's book The Great Physician's Rx for Health and Wellness and its seven keys; Current "101" courses include:

   * "Eating to Live 101"

   * "Whole Food Nutrition Supplements 101"

   * "Advanced Hygiene 101"

   * "Exercise and Body Therapies 101"

   * "Reducing Toxins 101"

   * "Emotional Health 101"

   * "Prayer and Purpose 101"

2. **FREE** resources (healthy recipes, what to E.A.T., resource guide)

3. **FREE** media--videos and video clips of Jordan, music therapy samples, etc.--and much more!

Additionally, Biblical Health Institute also offers in-depth courses for those who want to go deeper.

Course offerings include:

   * 40-hour certificate program to become a Biblical Health Coach

   * A la carte course offerings designed for personal study and growth

   * Home school courses developed by Christian educators, supporting home-schooled students and their parents (designed for middle school and high school ages)

For more information and updates on these and other resources go to
www.BiblicalHealthInstitute.com